Paris

Love, Loss and Longing in the City of Lights

WADDLE THE WORLD WITH RED PENGUIN BOOKS

Paris

All rights reserved.

Published by Emperor Books

Bellerose Village, New York

ISBN

Print 978-1-63777-488-5

Digital 978-1-63777-487-8

Contents

Paris Bench

DAVID LANGE

Ah, if the River Seine could only speak; the stories she would tell. Love and romance. Heartache and heartbreak. Intrigue and betrayal. Hope . . . and second chances.

Fog diffused the light from the lamp posts, lending a softness to the scene, as Peter, a middle-aged gentleman, buttoned his coat against the chill of an October evening in Paris. While lovers walked, hand in hand, along the banks of the Seine, Peter contented himself with his unobstructed view of the lovely river from his favorite bench. A statuesque woman in her mid-twenties approached. Lean and lovely, she might well have been a Paris fashion model, and Peter's mind raced for an explanation when she asked if she might join him on the bench. She spoke in English, but her enchanting French accent betrayed her national origin and clearly identified her as a native Parisian.

"You speak to me in English," said Peter. "For all the time I've spent in Paris, I thought I might have shaken the 'American tourist' look. Apparently not." The woman smiled and quickly sought to remedy any insult she might have unintentionally conveyed.

"Au contraire, you are looking very continental. I simply noticed the rolled newspaper at your side was in English and not French. As you were not reading the paper and looked rather lonely, I thought that perhaps I might join you. Of course, if I have disturbed your quiet reflections, then I sincerely apologize and shall leave you to your thoughts." Peter had, in fact, been dreamily reliving a very memorable moment from his younger days. However, the spell having been broken, he was not disinclined to accept the offer from the lovely stranger. Peter slid over to the right side of the bench and used his handkerchief to wipe the moisture from the painted wooden surface to his left.

"Please forgive my rudeness," said Peter. "Naturally, I welcome the company of a beautiful French woman." Peter snickered, amused by the seemingly preposterous notion that an attractive stranger, likely half his age, had somehow played the opening move of a romantic gambit. Peter got his first good look at the woman's face when she stepped around to the side of the bench. The soft glow of the nearby lamp revealed a heavenly visage like few he had ever seen before. Doe-eyed and radiant, the stranger stole Peter's breath away. His jaw dropped and he sat, in a veritable stupor, even as Lune reached out her hand in greeting, an enchanting smile stretching across her face, accentuated by her perfectly formed lips.

"Hi, I'm Lune," greeted the lovely stranger. Her smile faded a bit as Peter failed to respond in any fashion typically associated with sociable beings. Peter was stunned silent. It was not so much the great beauty of the woman he was speaking to as it was an eerie sense that they had met at some point in the past. The eyes. The smile. The voice. The gentle demeanor. All of it reminded him of Gabrielle. Still unable to form words, Peter desperately salvaged the moment by leaping to his feet and grasping Lune's soft hand with both his hands, holding them affectionately. Lune could see the effect she was having and nervously laughed, thanking Peter for the unspoken complement. Without question, Lune could have walked the fashion runways of Paris or Milan, had she chosen such a path in life, and so she was seldom shocked by the admiring gaze of men . . . but the look in Peter's eyes was something different. There was reverence and passion that went far beyond "I want to take you to bed tonight." Lune reached out with her other hand and Peter shifted his right hand to grasp it. They stood there, hand in hand, carefully scrutinizing one another. "Care to sit?" offered Lune, after the silence had transitioned from slightly awkward to uncomfortable and unsettling. Peter simultaneously released his grip on both Lune's hands, returning his own hands to the warm lined pockets of his trench coat.

"Yes. I'm so sorry. I'm not sure what came over me," responded Peter.

"Please don't apologize. Truly, I'm flattered," Lune replied, the beautiful smile returning to her face.

"You must think me a lecherous old man. I'm definitely not that. I'm a gentleman and a person of the highest moral character. The thing is . . . well . . . you look very much like someone I once knew; someone very special to me."

"Oh, and I thought that perhaps you were taken by my appearance," said Lune, more in jest than suffering any sense of disappointment. She was confident enough to know that good fortune had blessed her with attractive features. Peter considered a response and concluded that any course of action he might choose was fraught with peril so he simply returned to his spot on the bench, allowing room for Lune to sit beside him. Peter gazed out across the Seine towards the far bank which was only barely visible through the fog. The two sat together in silence, for a while, before Lune sought, once more, to strike up a conversation. "When I saw you sitting here on the bench, staring longingly upon our beautiful Seine, I thought to myself, *Now there's a man with a story to tell*."

"And are you the sort of woman who cares to waste part of her evening hearing the sorrowful tale of an old fool?" interjected Peter. Lune looked upon Peter with a sympathetic eye.

"I am always in the mood for a love story," responded Lune, her soft voice tearing down the walls that Peter had spent years building around his heart.

"So, you believe I am harboring a love story, do you? Perhaps I'm reflecting upon a tragic collision between two river cruise boats? Or, maybe, I'm considering some great financial loss—a failed business deal or unwise investment?" Lune mumbled something in French that Peter was unable to discern until she clearly repeated her words, in English.

"You have the look of one burdened by the blessing of love. I can tell," said Lune, her eyes sparkling. "I'd love to hear your story, if you're willing to share it with a stranger. Frankly, I don't see that there's much to lose from your perspective and it could well be that your story might provide me some life-enriching insights." Peter considered the request carefully before replying.

"There's nothing enriching about turning away from a once in a lifetime opportunity to share a future with the woman of your dreams. My story isn't a happy one."

"Please allow me to be the judge of that," said Lune. "Perhaps I may see your story in a different light. The story begins here, no?" Peter nodded, a little surprised by the bold yet completely accurate assertion.

"Yes. Right here at this bench."

"Was she beautiful?"

"No woman I had seen before nor since is her equal. Yes, she was very beautiful."

"And her name," asked Lune, resolved to limit her interruptions after the query.

"Gabrielle. Her name was Gabrielle."

"That's a lovely name," added Lune.

Peter paused, for a moment, and sighed. He had never shared this deeply personal and life-defining story with anyone and his brain was still working out how much of the tale he wished to surrender to a stranger. There was something disarming about Lune that persuaded him to open up. Somehow, he felt that she might understand and that she would not be quick to judge. Peter also had a strange feeling that this could be a first step toward relieving some of the painful heartache that had tormented him for over two decades.

"It was twenty-five years ago, today, that I was walking this very path along the bank of the Seine. I was studying architecture as an exchange student at the École Nationale Supérieure d'Architecture. Truth be told, I spent less time studying and more time drinking and socializing. My grades were not impressive and I was in jeopardy of losing my scholarship and having to return to the United States on account of poor academic performance. My parents were getting divorced, about the same time, and my world seemed to be spinning out of control. If I lost my scholarship, I'd have to put my college dreams on hold and return home to work in the factory. I'd seen my father part with all his life's ambitions and resign himself to being a wrench-turning ant in a nest of thousands at that factory and I knew I couldn't live like that. It was a very dark time in my life." Lune nodded, a concerned look on her face, but did not interrupt the storyteller. Peter fell silent for a minute, clearly trying to compose himself.

"And then came the 12th of October. I was walking along the bank of the Seine, as I often did when I needed time alone to reflect, when I noticed a woman hunched over and sobbing on a park bench—this park bench. I approached her, much as you approached me, and asked if I might lend assistance. When she turned toward me, eyes filled with tears, I knew she was the one. Our introductions were brief. Although I inquired, Gabrielle did not seem interested in sharing her problems. Rather than speak, we held hands and looked out upon the river. The moon was full that night—so bright and majestic that I could not help but believe there was some magic in the air. Moon beams shimmered across the water setting the entirety of the Seine ablaze in luminous splendor."

"How very romantic," added Lune, unable to resist the temptation as Peter set the stage for all that was to come.

"It was a perfect night for love to blossom. And it did. After a certain period of time, how long I cannot say as time lost all meaning that night, we began to converse. Gabrielle was a student, as well. She had recently lost her parents to a tragic accident and, while desperately searching for answers to her depression, fell into an abusive relationship with a controlling classmate who seemed, at the time, to be the answer to her grief. Before she knew it, she was trapped. Hooked on drugs and alcohol and dependent upon her boyfriend for lodging and basic necessities, she was all but a prisoner."

Tears began to stream from Lune's eyes as Peter told of Gabrielle's awful plight and how she contemplated suicide on several occasions to try to escape her pain.

"That is horrible," cried Lune. I've known several women who have similarly fallen into such a terrible trap and I might well have done so myself were it not for the excellent counsel my mother provided me while I was growing up. She warned me against such dependency and always made sure that I had a place to come home to if life failed to show me kindness."

"Consider yourself fortunate, Lune. Too many suffer the fate of dear Gabrielle. You owe your mother a great debt of gratitude for helping to spare you such pain by teaching you important lessons about self-worth, dignity, and true love."

"So, were you the knight in shining armor, riding in to save the day?"

"No. I wish I could have been. I'm afraid I was little more than a pleasant distraction. The magical moon fills your mind with all sorts of crazy notions. I began to believe that destiny had led me to my soul mate. I had never given much credence to the notion of soul mates until that evening. The moon also fooled me into believing that I was, somehow, worthy to possess this beautiful princess. I was so naïve—a boy chasing dreams."

"What's wrong with chasing dreams?" asked Lune.

"They can lead you down a dozen rabbit holes and distract you from doing the real work of living. That's what's wrong with chasing dreams?" Lune looked unconvinced.

"I'm not sure I agree . . . but please go on with your story. I want to know what happened next."

"Well, we enjoyed each other's company through the night and talked until the sun broke the horizon. We watched the beautiful sunrise and I think we both felt a certain lightness in our hearts. It was the dawn of a new day, both figuratively and literally."

"Although we were both very tired, neither of us wanted to part ways. We shared an irrational fear that the spell might be broken if either of us turned our back on the other. We didn't want the dream to end and so we held each other tightly, as if each of us were the life preserver keeping the other afloat in rough seas. We walked the streets of Paris, stopping at a quaint patisserie for crois-sants and coffee. After our morning snack, we continued on until we were too tired to speak intelligibly. That's when I invited Gabrielle to my apartment."

"And she agreed? I'm amazed she was so trusting of a stranger, especially after all she had been through."

"Yes. She agreed. I must admit, I was surprised, as well. I offered up my bed so that she could get some sleep because I was afraid of what she might be going home to, had I not. Perhaps an abusive and controlling boyfriend, infuriated that his property had spent the night away? I didn't know what awaited Gabrielle. I only knew that I needed to protect her from any possible retribution or maltreatment."

"And then you made love?" Lune asked, immediately regretting the leading question and her own impatience to find out how the story would progress. She readied herself for a rebuke that never came.

"No," said Peter. "Not that morning. Gabrielle did not want to be alone so we held hands, in bed, until she drifted off to sleep. My mind was alive with beautiful daydreams so I found it hard to sleep. Eventually, exhaustion caught up to me and I fell asleep, too."

"It was late afternoon when I finally awoke to the sound of the shower running in my small bathroom. Gabrielle's dress lay at the foot of the bed. By the time the water stopped, my heart was pounding out of my chest. I wish I could say my mind was focused on more noble endeavors but, in truth, lust had overcome my charitable aspirations. Alas, I was a mere man and no better."

"You shouldn't blame yourself for being that which you were born to be, Peter," added Lune. "There is nothing wrong with being a man and, if not for sexual attraction, our species would have gone extinct long before the birth of any saint." Peter blushed and looked away. He felt a little uneasy discussing sexual matters, more so given his audience was a young woman half his age. Lune assuaged his concerns and assured him that she was very interested to know how things progressed between the two. Resolving to modify his storytelling to keep the account at a PG rating, Peter continued on.

"After what seemed like an eternity, Gabrielle stepped back into the bedroom; the bath towel wrapped tightly around her body was barely large enough to conceal those parts best left to the imagination . . . at least on a first date. You know what I mean." Lune smiled at Peter's old-fashioned sense of propriety.

"I believe I do. But please go on."

"As you might imagine, I was speechless. Gabrielle's beauty had stolen my heart the night before but, somehow, with her makeup washed away and her short, wet hair wildly dancing about her forehead, she looked even more desirable than the painted doll I had spent the morning with. Gabrielle was a true natural beauty."

"And then you made love to her? asked Lune, a sly smile on her face.

"I wanted to. Well, part of me wanted to. But it just didn't seem right. Not yet. I wanted our relationship to be something special —something different. I didn't want to be just another one of the countless men who pursued beautiful women for a night's conquest. I thought I was better than that. I knew Gabrielle deserved better than that. No, I suggested that we might stroll along the Avenue des Champs-Élysées and then, later, find a nice restaurant for dinner. Gabrielle was concerned about wearing her now wrinkled dress out to a nice restaurant so I suggested we might go shopping for some new clothes."

"I'm impressed. She must have been grateful for your generosity?"

"I think she was surprised. In truth, I surprised myself. My rent for the month was already overdue and I knew the clothing and dinner would make a serious dent in my dwindling emergency savings. I wanted Gabrielle to believe I was successful and a good catch. I was anything but that. I had squandered my money on alcohol and diversions and I was on the verge of losing my scholarship. I painted myself to be this go-getter, on a fast track to become a rich corporate architect who would be designing and overseeing the construction of a veritable empire of luxurious skyscrapers across the globe. The sad part is, Gabrielle believed every word of it. I'll never forgive myself for misleading her in this way. I meant no harm. I was in love and I wanted Gabrielle to love me back. I could not believe that any woman would love me unless I was financially successful and moving aggressively toward achieving great things in life. I was a student, failing classes and failing in life."

"She may have known more than you suspected, Peter," said Lune, in a kind and assuring voice. "Women understand more than you might imagine."

"I don't know how she could have. In any case, I was so afraid to lose her that I tried very hard to be a better man. I escorted Gabrielle through several very posh department stores and she picked out a lovely dress, a jacket, and a few accessories."

"Expensive?" asked Lune.

"Actually, no. The items she chose were reasonably priced, especially given the stores we were visiting." Lune smiled, knowingly, reflecting on her earlier comment about women understanding more than they might let on.

"Eventually, we returned to the hotel and changed for dinner. I called up a taxi and we enjoyed a lovely meal at a five-star restaurant overlooking the Eiffel Tower. It was the most memorable meal of my life. Every detail was perfect and I could not have been more satisfied had I been dining with Venus, herself. After dinner, we walked to the Eiffel Tower and later caught a cab up to the Sacré-Cœur Basilica where we beheld a breathtaking view of the city lights. We held each other tightly, kissing as lovers do. Eventually, we returned to my apartment."

"And then you..."

"Yes. And then we made love. Our bodies moved as one, beneath the covers, and we both left the troubles of the world behind. Gabrielle responded to every touch, every gentle stroke of my fingers. Her pleasure became my measure of success for nothing else seemed to matter. Likewise, she took me to new heights— levels of ecstasy I never dreamed possible. One night turned into two, and then days became weeks. I completely forgot about my classes and school work. I was shocked back into reality when the phone rang, one afternoon, while Gabrielle was out shopping for a baguette, cheese, and wine for our evening in. It was the Financial Aid Office calling to inform me that my scholarship had been revoked and that I was to be expelled from school. I was devastated. So much for living in a dream, right? Reality had finally grabbed me by the throat and I felt starved for air. I had shared my hopes and aspirations with Gabrielle and she believed in me. I panicked. I didn't know what to do. It was Christmas Eve and I was at the end of my rope. I used what little funds I had left to purchase an airline ticket back to the United States with just enough money left to buy a few gifts for Gabrielle and cover the cost of a holiday dinner at a nice restaurant."

"She knew something wasn't right, didn't she?"

"I'm sure she suspected. I've never been a good actor and I certainly didn't feel right about continuing a charade. But I also couldn't bear the thought of breaking the news to Gabrielle on Christmas Eve. So, we went to dinner. We exchanged gifts. We made love. We each played our roles, uneasily, in this final scene. We spent Christmas day together. We held each other more tightly and kissed more deeply. The next morning, I crept away, leaving only a note of apology as an admission of my cowardice and my failure."

"How awful. That must have been heartbreaking."

"I've had to live with the shame these past twenty-five years. I was never worthy of Gabrielle. What she saw in me, I'll never know. It was wrong of me to seek a place in her life. She was the sun in the sky and I was..." Peter stopped abruptly, unable to continue his tale as emotions overtook him. He fought hard to regain his composure, wiping tears away with his handkerchief. "Heartbreaking? Yes. Absolutely heartbreaking. But, ever since returning to the U.S., I vowed that I would become a better man. I would become that man that I had led Gabrielle to believe I was."

"Did you return to the factory? The factory your father had worked in?"

"I did, but only briefly. I kept my nose to the grindstone and worked multiple jobs to help pay my way through college. I first earned my bachelor's degree and later obtained a master's degree in Architecture. But I wasn't simply focused on academic and professional excellence. I truly wanted to better myself as a person. Never again did I lie or seek to deceive others. I regularly donated my time to several charities assisting victims of domestic abuse and swore that I would do everything in my power to help promote healthy relationships so that no one would have to endure the pain that Gabrielle went through."

"A noble cause, Peter, but I'm afraid you've set an impossible goal. You are dreaming again, my friend."

"Perhaps," Peter said, smiling through his tears. Maybe there's still a bit of a dreamer left in me." Lune smiled and reached over to squeeze Peter's hand.

"We all need to dream. We all need to keep hope alive." Peter squeezed Lune's hand in return. They both looked back towards the river. The fog was thinning and the Seine was now brilliantly illuminated beneath a full moon.

"Peter, did you ever marry? Do you have a family?" Peter sighed.

"You know, I tried a few times. I mean, I tried to build relationships but nothing seemed right after Gabrielle. I couldn't let go. Or, maybe, I just didn't want to let go. I know, that's kind of sad, isn't it?" Lune considered Peter's words.

"You still love her that much?"

"Yup. I still love her that much. I gave up what I loved most in this world because I felt I had nothing to offer beyond pain and disappointment. I was sure that a beautiful woman like Gabrielle would find her way and make something of herself. I would have been like an old rusty anchor that pulled her down. I couldn't bear to do that to her. I loved her too much. I love her too much."

"Please don't be offended by what I say but I think you've put too much weight on what you were feeling when, perhaps, you should have given more consideration to what Gabrielle felt. It's possible she saw through all the smoke and mirrors. It's possible that she knew exactly who you were—your vulnerabilities and insecurities . . . but also your strengths and the goodness within your heart; a goodness you too readily deny. Did you consider that Gabrielle may have loved you simply for who you were and how you made her feel?" Lune's words struck deeply and were met with a contemplative silence followed by a stream of tears.

"You're right, Lune. I was self-centered and I was wrong. I found true love and I let it go. And now, I willingly serve my penance for my greatest mistake."

"And is penitence what brings you back to this bench?" asked Lune.

"No. Not penitence. Love. Love brings me back. Every year I return to this bench and I remember a love so pure and true that it erases all the sorrows and woe within my heart. It revives my spirit and reminds me of what is good in this world. That's what keeps me coming back. Love.

Lune began weeping and she slid closer to Peter and wrapped her arms around him giving him a big hug that caught him totally off guard.

"I love you, Dad!"

"What?" Peter replied, bewildered and unsure of what he had just heard. Lune repeated her words, slowly and clearly.

"I...love...you,...Dad."

"Dad?"

"Yes. I was named "Lune" in homage to the beautiful full moon that you enjoyed with my mother on the night you first met."

"Then you are my daughter!" Peter returned the hug, tenfold, nearly squeezing the air out of Lune's lungs. "Please tell me, how is your mother? Is she well? Is she happy?" The excitement in Peter's voice was palpable and Lune couldn't help but laugh as she wiped away the remaining tears from her cheeks.

"Mom, I think you better take it from here," said Lune, further adding to Peter's confusion. He looked at Lune, quizzically, and she swept her long black hair away from her right ear revealing a small wireless earpiece connected via Wi-Fi to her phone.

"What's going on here, Lune?" asked Peter, more confused than ever.

"I'm sorry, Dad. I didn't know how else to do this."

"To do what, Lune?"

"Well, you see, I've witnessed you re-visiting this spot for several years now. Mom visits it, too. Sometimes, we've both watched you together. I kept telling Mom that she should walk over and talk to you but she felt you wouldn't want to see her, that somehow it would cause you pain or make you sad She used to say that a good-looking man like you would surely be married by now and that it wouldn't be right for her to stir up a bunch of memories. You know—leave the past in the past. I tried to tell her that you probably wouldn't be making a yearly pilgrimage to this spot if..." Lune stopped abruptly when she saw her mother emerging from behind a distant tree. Lune's phone had been transmitting the whole time and Gabrielle had heard every heart-felt word of the conversation on the bench.

Gabrielle approached, slowly, and stepped into the light of the nearby lamppost. Peter followed Lune's gaze over toward the lamp and his heart nearly stopped when he saw Gabrielle. Peter quickly got up and, being in such a hurry to close the distance between himself and Gabrielle, tripped on one of the legs of the bench and fell upon the soft grass. Gabrielle gasped and raced over to him. Whether due to a release of nervous energy or because of the child-like glee filling his heart, Peter lay there laughing in the grass. Gabrielle knelt down to attend to him and, after seeing the expression of pure joy on Peter's face, began to laugh, as well.

Gabrielle was the first to speak. "I always told Lune that if we ever met again, you'd surely fall for me just like our first night beneath that beautiful moon. I just didn't think you'd fall this hard." Gabrielle reached for Peter's hand and they laughed together.

"Gabrielle, did you hear our entire conversation?" Peter asked, once the laughter had died down. Gabrielle's hair was still short, looking much as it did when they first met. She reached up and slowly pulled the Wi-Fi earpiece from her ear and slid it into her jacket pocket. Peter recognized the jacket. It was the one he had bought for Gabrielle before their first dinner together. Though well-worn, it still looked great on her. Rather than answer Peter's question directly, Gabrielle leaned over and kissed Peter passionately where he lay on the grass. Beneath the light of the magical moon, Gabrielle appeared to have aged little since the last time the two lovers had embraced. Or, perhaps, it wasn't the magic of the moon at all. Love creates its own special magic.

The fog, much like the weight of regret and disappointment, dissipated completely. Gabrielle reclined on the grass next to Peter and the two gazed up toward the moon and the stars while holding hands. Lune got up from the bench, satisfied that she had done something good, and prepared to leave her parents so that they might make up for lost time or simply frolic in the grass to their heart's content. As she walked away, she called out "Will I see you for breakfast?" Her parents just laughed.

"Maybe not tomorrow," replied Gabrielle. Lune smiled.

"Okay, well, please be sure to send me a wedding invitation, then." Faint, giggles was all Lune heard in reply. She walked away with a big grin on her face.

Peter and Gabrielle did not make breakfast the next morning. Several months later, Lune received a wedding invitation and, on October 12th, twenty-six years after the day they first met, Peter and Gabrielle were married in a small ceremony along the banks of the Seine.

The End

WILLIAM JOHN ROSTRON

He sidled up to the bar and ordered the first of many drinks he would consume that night. He intended to spend the night alone, choosing not to be with his girlfriend Pam or anyone else. There was no joy in his attitude, merely resignation to his fate. It was a fate that had been determined four years before.

"James, another?" asked the bartender of the small tavern on the corner of Rue Beautreillis in central Paris.

"You know, Jean-Pierre, people don't call me James."

"Would you rather I call you Buddy or some such other nickname that you Americans are so fond of. We Parisiennes prefer the formality or the class of a proper Christian name."

"If that floats your boat, then call me James."

"So, James, what are your plans for tomorrow's holiday?"

"I didn't realize that you celebrated our holiday? How American of you, Jean-Pierre."

"Do not forget that you Americans would not be independent if we French did not help you with your quest. So, the 4th of July is very much our holiday, too."

"Then you can have it. I give it to you. I could care less. I am enjoying Paris and the freedom from the shitty laws that keep me tied down in America. If I lose my appeal there, I go to jail. Therefore, I will probably be here forever...and I mean that quite literally." An all-knowing smile came across James' face.

Then, James viewed a suavely-dressed, elderly man from the corner of his eye. His neatly-trimmed beard framed a face distinguished by a pair of piercing eyes. His three-piece black suit was in line with 1971 Paris couture. The cane he used appeared to be a prop, simply to add an air of importance to his movements. He sidled his way over to the bar, dismissing James' desire to wallow in his solitude.

"Mind if I join you?"

"Yes, I do mind," whispered the young man, barely looking up from his fourth Jack Daniels.

"You didn't say that when we first met four years ago."

"I'd remember if I ever met someone like you."

"I don't always look the same—one of the skills I am particularly proud of having developed."

The younger man looked closely into the face of the stranger, and he knew. In reality, he had known for at least eight months that this moment would come. Until then, he had convinced himself that their encounter four years prior had been a dream, an illusion, perhaps the results of a bad peyote trip. But recently, he had come to realize that it had happened.

Ten months earlier, in September 1970, Jimi Hendrix had died of a drug overdose. James had been friends with the guitarist, and indeed they shared something in common that few would ever know about. James had been a struggling lead singer of a little-known group when he met the extraordinary guitarist in Mississippi one night in 1967. First, they had gotten high together. Then Hendrix had convinced him to ride down to a place that Jimi only referred to as "The Crossroads." There, he had done the unthinkable—something that had not seemed real at the time. However, its reality had been proven time and time again over the last few years. At the urging of Hendrix, he had made a deal with the devil for stardom. Unfortunately, the price had been his immortal soul.

Stardom came knocking on his door, and his unknown band became world-famous within months. Wealth and adoration followed. However, he rarely acknowledged the suspected supernatural origins of his success. He worried that something was amiss when Brian Jones, the leader of the Rolling Stones, died at 27 years old. And then his friend Jimi died at 27. James had not only been to the "Crossroads" with his departed friend but he had been made aware that Jones had also been there. Who could argue with the fame that the Rolling Stones had achieved? Yet it had taken Janis Joplin to figure the whole thing out.

He had met the singer during a chance encounter years before. At that time, he had told her about his hallucination at "The Crossroads." Not having yet had any personal success with her career, she had been interested. However, it was not until Hendrix's memorial service in September 1970 that James ran into Janis again. It was then that the two of them realized the truth.

The paparazzi recorded the altercation that he had with Joplin. The public found it amusing that two great stars should have a violent confrontation over seemingly nothing. Unfortunately, those reporters were not privy to the conversation between the two.

"Janis, wait! We have to talk. Talk about...you know...about Jimi."

"It's too late, you idiot. You told me about "The Crossroads," and.... Well, what do you think happens now? What happened to Brian? What happened to Jimi?"

"Yeah, but it could be years. Who knows?" She looked at him in disbelief. He didn't want to see the truth.

"You still don't get it. Brian Jones died at 27. Jimi died at 27. And god-dammit, if we had done our research, we would have realized that the whole "Crossroads" thing started with the blues great, Robert Johnson, who spoke and even sang about going down to the "Crossroads"...and he died at 27."

"You're just being hysterical."

"I'll show you who's being hysterical." Joplin took a bottle of Southern Comfort, smashed it over his head, and rode away.

Janis Joplin died three weeks after Jimi Hendrix in October of 1970 at age 27.

The sophisticated gentleman pointed to the young man.

"It's time. Would you like a little heroin to ease your journey, James?"

He shrugged his shoulders at the older man and finished his Jack Daniels.

The older gentleman giggled. "I just can't resist."

"Resist what?"

"The punchline."

"Punchline?"

"Come, James...it's time for me to light your fire."

James "Jim" Morrison's premature death in Paris remains obscured by mystery, rumor, and conspiracy theories about his demise. The death certificate stated heart failure, but no autopsy was ever performed. He was 27.

There are poets and artists among the great and the good in Père Lachaise cemetery, where he was buried. Molière, Delacroix, Edith Piaf, and Morrison's idol, Oscar Wilde, all lie nearby the grave of the legendary singer of The Doors. Despite the other legends surrounding him, Jim Morrison's final resting place remains the main tourist attraction of Pere Lachaise cemetery.

- The above is a work of fiction. However, it is based on specific actual incidents.
- Jim Morrison died in Paris on July 3, 1971. This was exactly two years to the day after Brian Jones drowned in a pool at age 27.
- If and when he returned to America, he faced jail in Miami for an indecent exposure conviction.
- Morrison spent his last day on Rue Beautreillis in central Paris.
- Though no one ever explained the reason for the altercation between Jim Morrison and Janis Joplin, it did happen. Joplin cracked a bottle of Southern Comfort over Morrison's head in a fit of drunken anger.
- Jimi Hendrix rose from the relative obscurity playing to a small club (Café Wha?) audience in Greenwich Village to superstardom in a matter of months.
- Janis Joplin thought of returning home to Texas because of her failure to break into the music business before

becoming the most renowned female singer of her generation.

- The Doors toiled without economic or artistic success for two years before their first hit, "Light My Fire."
- Jimi Hendrix and Jim Morrison knew each other well.
- Thousands of people visit Jim Morrison's Paris grave each year.
- And finally, the coincidence of the deaths of so many musical artists at 27 remains an unexplained coincidence. It has garnered significant ink from writers much more talented than me and is often referred to as the "27 Club."

The 27 Club Membership Roll

The Board of Directors:

Robert Johnson (1938) – is considered by many the greatest blues guitarist of all time.

Brian Jones (1969) – guitarist and founder of the Rolling Stones

Jimi Hendrix (1970) – is considered by many as the most original guitarist of the 1960s

Janis Joplin (1970) – Perhaps the most significant female singer of the 1960s

Jim Morrison (1971) – Lead singer of the Doors

Kurt Cobain (1994) – Founder, lead singer, and guitarist of Nirvana. Icon of "Grunge Rock."

Amy Winehouse (2011) – Award-winning British Pop/Blues singer

OTHER MEMBERS:

Rudy Lewis (1964) – Vocalist for the Drifters

Malcolm Hale (1968) – Founding member and lead guitarist for Spanky and Our Gang

Dickie Pride (1969) – British Rock and Roll singer

Alan "Blind Owl" Wilson (1970) – Lead singer of Canned Heat

Ron "Pigpen" McKernan (1973) – Founding member, keyboardist, and singer of Grateful Dead

Pete Ham (1975) – lead vocalist of 1970s rock band Badfinger

And dozens of others from various genres of music.

A Museum Piece

KEN GOLDMAN

"Oh, they loved dearly; their souls kissed, they kissed with their eyes, they were both but one single kiss!"

~Heinrich Heine, German Poet

As field trips went, this one to the Museum of Natural History so far had proven lame. What could you really say about the breeding habits of the Alaskan sea otter that would moisten the panties of any seventeen year old schoolgirl? The twenty St. Clotilde students concluded their tour with a visit to the popular Human Oddities wing, and finally the museum showed some promise. The girls gazed at two skulls conjoined at the jaw and preserved behind glass. The golden identification plate offered little more information than the French names belonging to the skeletal heads.

Someone asked, "Were these Siamese twins or something?"

The young tour guide's name tag read BELINDA, and she held a special place in her heart for this grotesque anomaly, especially since the past summer. On some days she kidded her younger guests that the exhibition piece had been used as a paperweight by Marilyn Manson, then quickly moved on with the tour. Today she felt like talking. "These are the skulls of Francoise La Bourliere and her paramour Antoine Furois, Parisian sweethearts of the French aristocracy, dead nearly fifty years who met their end one spring morning as they strolled along the Seine. Their story is clouded by inaccuracies and exaggeration, but I can detail a pretty faithful version. Want to hear?" Belinda had developed a respectable flair for the dramatic on this job, and her voice dropped a pitch. "Do you young ladies believe in magic?"

Most of the group nodded, but not Suzanne. Wearing a fashionable red scrunchie that offset her starched parochial school uniform, the pretty disbeliever decisively shook her head. "Magic is crap. It didn't work so well for Siegfried and Roy, did it?"

A wise assed kid. Every school group had its junior iconoclast, and kids seething with angst were Belinda's favorites. Not long ago she had been one of them. She beaded in on Suzanne.

"Then maybe you believe in passion? You see, Antoine desired Francoise from the moment he first saw her. Fearing she might not return his affection, he -"Belinda paused to look over her shoulder. This part of her narrative could be delicate if the school's dour nuns lurked nearby. The bad little girl living inside her was alive and well. Five years out of Holy Savior and she still checked to see if the Sisters were watching. "... he procured the services of a sorceress named Amelie who might encourage the young woman's favor. Although Amelie was as hideous as Francoise was beautiful, after one hour spent with the young and wealthy monsieur she was determined to have him for herself." "Did she cast a spell on him?" one grossly overweight student asked the guide. The more homely school kids usually seemed the most interested in knowing about the power of magic spells. Maybe those who were themselves different needed to believe in witchery the most.

Belinda slipped into tourspeak mode. "Even the best magic is never fool proof. But Amelie cast no spell on Antoine he hadn't selected for himself. The woman understood her blackest magic was a poor substitute for true love, and she refused to use it to win Antoine's affection. Correctly intuiting matters of the heart, she offered the smitten man a vial containing a strong potion of exotic and forbidden herbs. If lovers sipped the vial's contents, she instructed, afterward the liquid allowed each of them one wish pertaining to the other."

The heavyset school girl frowned. "That wasn't very smart of the sorceress if Amelie wanted Antoine for herself." Belinda smiled. This kid needed a few more years to grasp a clear understanding of the evil intentions of which women were capable.

"The most clever woman never lets on that she is. The sorceress believed that behind all male desire lurks a consuming need to possess. Amelie knew Antoine would desire Francoise to be his forever, and Francoise's assurance of eternal fidelity would likely become his one wish. That meant for the rest of his days the woman would cling to her lover like an itching garment. In time the sorceress knew Antoine would return to her little shop an exhausted man, begging for release from a constant lover who allowed him no rest. Amelie would offer the poor man relief, of course. He would be in her debt, and then she would have him."

This part of the story stirred memories, and the guide glanced toward the entranceway where the museum's dark-haired curator stood, Geoffrey B. Haskin, whose family had a considerable financial interest in the place. Belinda quickly looked away. She noticed the girl with the red scrunchie was watching him too, and why not? He was a real looker, there was no denying that. But Belinda's narrative was not meant for a man's ears, especially this man's. "The next morning Antoine persuaded Francoise to meet him at a small café, the revolving Tuileries Carousel along the Seine. When a particularly beautiful swan distracted the young woman, he sipped some of the sorceress' potion, then emptied the remainder into Francoise's tea. The results were instantaneous. The longing expression in his woman's eyes encouraged the suitor to waste no time in speaking his heart. He insisted he would never leave her, adding he had but one desire—to hear those same words from her. Smothering him with kisses, the smitten Francoise readily whispered them. And so, one wish had been uttered and granted.

"Hand in hand they walked the path along the Left Bank, each hopelessly immersed in love for the other, stopping frequently to steal a kiss along the way. The further they walked, the more passionate their kisses became.

"The potion's effects had almost expired when Antoine, hoping to benefit from the full effects of the sorceress' brew, whispered, 'My love, today you have granted me my greatest wish. If you had one wish you would ask of me, what would that be?' Francoise didn't hesitate telling him 'I wish I could go on kissing you forever!' Too overtaken with the moment, the man hadn't realized the tragic portent of his lover's desire until she pressed her parted lips to his. Their mouths immediately became one skin impossible to separate. Stealing one another's breath with every inhale, the two struggled ridiculously to break free of their death kiss. Attempts to scream made matters worse. Onlooking strollers pointed and laughed, misunderstanding what terrible thing had occurred. The lovers' end came quickly, and I suppose that was fortunate. Even in death, no one could divide them. Each had their wish and here are their skulls to tell you about it."

Suzanne scrunched her face. "Ewwwwwwwww!"

"There's a little postscript to this story, but it's kind of personal. You guys interested?"

The girls' nods were unanimous.

"Last summer following senior year in college I was nursing a broken heart of my own. I visited Paris, losing myself in walks along the Seine and sipping wine in a dozen outdoor cafés with exotic names like Deux Magots and La Coupole along the Left Bank, making my way along the Saint-Germain-Des-Pre in the fashionable district of Montparnasse. By accident I came upon a small shop run by an old woman who called herself Madame Amelie. She was even uglier than I imagined, her troll-like hideousness compounded by an extremely ungraceful old age that had transformed the woman into a hag. Waiting until the shop emptied, I approached her.

"'Francoise La Bourliere and Antoine Furois, Madame. Do you know these names?'" I asked in the poorest French ever uttered. The woman didn't bat an eye. But finally she spoke.

"'Mademoiselle, few Parisians of my years have not heard those names.' The Madame was, of course, correct. In its day the bizarre story had spread throughout France. But word of mouth had distorted the truth, and over time the tale became regarded as fiction among most clear thinking Frenchmen. Deciding to be more direct I handed the old woman a fistful of francs. After examining the money, she looked closely at me.

'Qu'est-ce que c'est?'

"'Madame Amelie, I know the story of those doomed lovers. I know about your role in it.' I could see the woman had become agitated and required some assurance of my intentions. 'I have no reason to judge you, Madame. In fact, I'm very glad to have found you. You see, there is a matter that concerns my own heart.'

"I explained to the old woman about a young man who recently had lied to me, one day promising love and the next deciding he had tired of me. Knowing he had broken my heart, he pursued another woman before my eyes. If the sorceress' potion could salvage what remained of the man's love for me - or at least help me get over mine - I assured her I would someday return to Paris with several additional fists full of francs.

"'Men talk a fine game, Mademoiselle. They speak quite freely of forevers.' That's all she muttered before disappearing into her parlor to mix a batch of her magic. She returned within a few minutes, impatient to send me on my way. I understood why."

"I wondered if maybe I were doing the right thing, questioned whether I'd been foolish to even believe in magic or sorcery. But when I returned home I slipped the potion into the man's coffee and decided from that moment I was done with him. And, happily, I am! So maybe there *is* something to be said for magic, huh?"

Belinda savored the moment of triumph she had created, but a shrill voice interrupted her rumination. Another group of museum visitors stood waiting in their queue while their pissed off guide shuffled about with nothing to do. The blonde woman displayed a noticeable hobble in her step as if this job had required too much time spent on her feet.

"Let's move it, Belinda! How about wrapping it up so my group can see some of the exhibits too before closing time?"

"Sorry, Lydia. We're moving right now. Okay girls, you heard the nice lady!" A peaches and cream smile emerged, although some of the cream had gone sour. "That limp looks like it's getting pretty bad. Maybe someone should look at it."

Managing her own affected smile that displayed a complete lack of warmth, the blonde steered her group quickly past Belinda whose own smile suggested something much worse.

Suzanne had watched the mini drama unfold. It was like playing connect the dots when she had been little. Already her brain penciled in the spaces to form a picture, and the picture included three people. The good looking man in the museum appeared too well dressed for a museum worker, and he had been standing in that same spot too long to be a tourist. Suzanne had seen enough t.v. soapers to recognize a lovers' triangle when she spotted one, but she said nothing to her classmates. Instead she approached her tour guide with one huge shit eating grin as if she had solved an incredible math equation.

"That well dressed man over there... and that blonde tour guide? Are they—?"

Belinda winked at Suzanne in the universal language shared among all women. Suzanne watched as her guide approached the man, the girl inching closer to listen for whatever further drama unfolded. She knew this was eavesdropping, an act that would earn her sore knuckles if Sister Agatha saw. She didn't care.

"Hello, Geoffrey," Belinda said, but she pronounced it JEFF-rey as if making some kind of point.

The man said nothing.

"Something wrong? Cat got your tongue?"

Face contorted, seeming pained and confused, he managed to speak.

"Heh-wo, Beh-wij-a ..."

It seemed he had tried to say 'Hello Belinda,' but what came out resembled nothing like that. He sounded like someone who had taken diction lessons from Elmer Fudd, his speech impediment so pronounced several St. Clotilde girls standing nearby stifled giggles. Suzanne thought that seemed cruel enough, but felt especially bewildered by her tour host's harsh greeting when she must have been aware of the poor guy's disadvantage. Suzanne would have questioned Belinda about that, but Sister Agatha wanted the girls inside the bus for the return trip to St. Clotilde's, so goodbyes were hasty. Suzanne said nothing to Belinda nor to anyone else, selecting a seat apart from the others.

Some dots refused to connect. The girl continued working events over in her head thirty minutes later as the bus entered the Interstate and her classmates had joined together in a singing pop chorus of Britney Spears crap. Something was missing, all right, something no one had detected. Suzanne rewound her mind's video of the past hour.

Lydia, the other woman.

["That limp looks like it's getting pretty bad."]

... and the handsome and dapper lover who could hardly speak Belinda's name as if ...

["Cat got your tongue?"]

Something in that ... yes, something only Belinda knew.

[The most clever woman never lets on that she is.]

... and maybe there *is* something to be said for magic.

What had Belinda said were Francoise's last words to Antoine?]

"I wish I could go on kissing you forever ..."

[Forever ...]

Something else ... something else from Amelie the hag ...

"Men talk a fine game, Mademoiselle. They speak quite freely of forevers."

Talk ...

Hello, JEFF-rey. Cat got your tongue?

["Heh-wo, Beh-wij-a ..."]

... Kiss ... Tongue ...

French kissing ... or something else? Something ...

... dirtier?

[Cat got your tongue?]

Cat ... kitten ... puss-puss ...

Puss-Puss got your tongue ...???

Suzanne bolted forward in her seat. While the school bus filled with song, in her mind's eye the young and handsome man was kissing blonde Lydia, all right. But not on her lips, oh no, not on her lips at all, but somewhere else... somewhere else where the cat had gotten his tongue. And kept it too!

... down there!!!

[Forever!]]

["That limp looks like it's getting pretty bad."]

Suzanne's face contorted with disgust. Nearby her schoolmates stopped singing and

turned to stare when she squealed.

"Ewwwwwwwwwwwwwwwwww ... ."

A view from my croissant

HANNA SWANEPOEL

A life on the roll was never expected
around a croissant beside a spoon
slowly snailing upwards, this croissant mountain

A view over my beloved Paris,
the walkers-by with their portrait painting trophies
A sport perhaps eating escargot
I'm on a roll
Away from the sidewalk
Down the rûe
Parfumerie on my left a wondrous smell
But I am slow

Thought I'll make it to the bridge where locks are sealed and
secrets kept
The sight of the cuisine
The long French loaf too steep to climb
I'll pass, but in a hurry not to be seen
The balcony flowers call,
At last I am home
Sunset
Oh the view from my croissant,
And the life of an Escargot

Ahh, Paris

PATRICIA CONOR HODAPP

In Paris for a job interview, I had free days to myself. I quickly ingratiated myself with Julien the concierge at my hotel and found macarons were a great bargaining chip.

Overhearing the American hiring team mentioning that they had a view of the Eiffel Tower from their hotel room, I stowed that nugget of information away. I had no such view.

Later the hiring team bragged about their lunch at Le Jules Verne in the Eiffel Tower and commiserated with me that to enjoy a meal there I would have needed to have planned weeks, if not months, in advance to get a reservation. I took that as a challenge.

Approaching my hotel concierge Julien with macarons that I had just purchased when the local patisserie had opened, I humbly asked if he might secure me a reservation at Le Jules Verne, that day or any day in the following week. He looked at me in horror. My high school French is far from comprehensive, but I could see that his was a true apology and then shaking his head said quietly, "Non, non, non. Impossible." I thanked him and said I would be back by 11:30am, should anything become available. I saw his stare of disbelief that I had even requested such an impossible task.

Arriving back at the hotel at 11:45pm, I was greeted by a mildly hysterical hotel general manager and Julien. My shopping bags were taken from me and I was rushed into a taxi. They informed me that my lunch reservation was for noon. Not to delay!

Arriving at the Eiffel Tower, the elevator ride to Le Jules Verne was brief. Greeted by the maître d', I was quickly seated on a plush chair at a two person table by the windows. Around me were elegantly dressed customers, who obviously had planned on lunch at Le Jules Verne.

My waiter introduced himself as Martin, suggested a prosecco and brought me a menu. Nothing was too far out of my budget, so I settled in for the treat of a great meal while overlooking Paris. The scallops were superb and the attention Martin gave me made me feel very special. As I waited for my appetizer, I pulled out my sketch book and started sketching the view and the people in the restaurant. When Martin appeared with the scallops, he inquired, "Are you an artist?" I just said I liked to sketch and paint and these are to capture my memories. After showing him my sketches, he called the maître d' over to see my drawings, which included ones of him and the waiters waiting to serve their customers. He was delighted with my little sketches.

Soon I found all of the waiters coming to see my sketches and each one brought a sample of a menu item for me. It was a small parade of unexpected treats!

The elegant couple to my right called the waiter over to ask, "Who is she?" And he replied imperiously, "An American artist." A title I shall long cherish.

What a joyful time. With my coffee came a small silver box with chocolates and langues de chat cookies.

I probably overstayed my reservation time, but no one came to hurry me out. I lingered and chatted with the waiters, all of whom wanted to know more about America. They personally escorted me to the elevator and pointed out special points of interest as I waited. With hugs all around, I departed.

Upon entering the hotel, the manager Patrick and Julien the concierge came to greet me and asked if I had enjoyed Le Jules Verne. I was still so thrilled over my fabulous experience, I just beamed at them and said it was magnificent!

Realizing the hiring team was leaving in the morning, but I had one more night, I once again approached the manager. I told Patrick if I could have their room for the one night, I would clear out my room immediately and they did not have to clean the other room. The hiring team was all women whom I had known for several years. The manager at first protested. I then stated perhaps I could not afford a room with a view of the Eiffel Tower and thanked him for even entertaining my wildly impertinent request.

As the hiring team departed after lunch, I entered the lobby to find Patrick waiting for me. "Allow my bell captain to assist you. He will come to your room in half an hour to receive your bags." I again protested that I could not afford a room with an Eiffel Tower view, and he waved me off.

That night I left my curtains open to enjoy the magical lights of the Eiffel Tower. After midnight, I set my alarm for 1:00 am and woke to check if the lights had changed color. Then I did the same each hour until dawn. The lights remained the same color, but the Tower outlined against the dawn was magical.

I have not been back to Paris, but in some ways I do not believe I could have had a more exciting and magical time ever again. Merci, Paris.

Alter Egos

DAVID CLÉMENCEAU

Become who you are

PART 1

Growing up, Marie hated the place where she and her mother lived together in a fifteen-storey building in one of the many social housing projects that surrounded Paris. People who did not live there and only heard about these *banlieues* in the news mistakenly tended to believe that the southern suburbs of the French capital were not as bad as the northern ones. Marie felt that they were wrong. It was obvious to her that living in the projects was bad anywhere in the world. She also hated people talking wisely about matters they didn't have a clue about to begin with. Those who pretended to know better simply illustrated their flagrant lack of knowledge in the matter, on top of their inability to keep their ignorance to themselves.

She and her mother, Aline, lived in a small flat which had only two rooms, one of which being the living room where her mother slept on a convertible couch. The only real room was Marie's. Although she was only eleven years old, she had a solid understanding of the circumstances that surrounded her life and her mother's. She was convinced that all children who lived in her neighbourhood and in the adjacent buildings had that very same grasp of reality but lost it during adolescence to society's expectations towards them – or, the way Marie saw it, to the country's heartless economic working-class engine that steadily and relentlessly ground every single one of its cogs into dust, only to see them replaced by the next generation.

Aline worked six days a week at a hairdresser's and often did house calls for friends and neighbours on Sundays. Maurine, the only neighbour they knew on the same floor, was one of her clients and the two women had a mutual agreement. Being a fortune teller, Maurine sometimes read people's fortunes with tarot cards in her spare time. And whenever she told Aline her fortune, Maurine was happy to get her hair done in return, free of charge. It was a sensible arrangement since, out of principle, Maurine never asked for payment for reading someone's cards. It was, however, common knowledge and understood for all her clients that no work should remain unpaid. Therefore, people always made a donation, either in money, usually a small, symbolic sum, or in goods such as a pack of flour or a home cooked meal. The difference with Aline was that their exchange was set at a fixed price.

Sometimes Marie's mother and their neighbour spent some of their off time together, having coffee or just chatting and, on occasion, even went out together. During a conversation, while Marie had been waiting patiently by her mother's side, she overheard that Maurine was of Irish origins. Her name was a variation of Marie's own, but the girl never noticed a surname (although she could have sworn that Maurine must have had one). When asked about where in Ireland Maurine was from, she just said evasively that her mother was born in a travelling community called Tinkers.

Judging from the woman's appearance, the girl decided that Maurine had to be about the same age as her mother, who was forty. Strangely enough, Marie had felt somehow connected to the dark-haired, pale woman next-door ever since she and her mother met her for the first time. Moreover, and as far as Marie could tell, Maurine was the closest thing she knew her mother had to a friend.

Since Aline earned just enough to pay for the bills and buy food, when Marie wanted pocket money for things her mother wouldn't buy her (or couldn't afford), she had to work for it. So when Mrs Aliagas, an elderly widow who lived on the ninth floor, just below Marie's and Aline's flat, needed some groceries, Marie went with her to help her pick the items she wanted and carry the bag back up to her flat. When Mrs Aliagas was too tired or aching from arthritis, she sent Marie to go on her own. The old lady always gave Marie five euros, once back at her place. She was kind, though rough around the edges, always swearing, and wore glasses as thick as bottlenecks. Marie often marvelled at how they didn't fall off her steep, freckled nose from their sheer weight. Marie also thought that it was a terrible thing to be so old and helpless; with no one else to look after you.

Little Marie also walked the elderly Dariot couple's pug, Hector. She hated dogs, too, but it was easy money to walk the stupid mutt around the courtyard until it had thoroughly urine-poisoned even the most resilient samples of suburban flora and dropped a couple of lengthy turds on the concrete walkway, right next to the dried-out flower patches and nettles. No one really cared anyway. People kept their children indoors after nightfall. Then, youths and small-time gangsters took possession of the benches and the entrances to the tower blocks.

Marie didn't like it when it got dark. Not that she liked it any better in the daytime. But she struggled to accept the commonly used adage stating *that's* how it was. If that was truly the case, she contended that *it* sucked tremendously.

Since she was a small child, Marie had always thought of herself as being different from the other children in her neighbourhood and at school, and usually preferred to keep to herself. She enjoyed learning, which made it somehow easier for her classmates to ostracise her – and ultimately leave her alone. No one around Marie, including her mother, understood how anyone could enjoy learning. She relished the thought in advance of going to school the next day to learn. And despite her mother's failure to understand her daughter in many other aspects, Aline understood that Marie was not like the other children, perhaps even special (although she didn't have a clear notion as to what exactly that implied). She knew, though, that her daughter liked to read. Therefore, Aline came home from work early every Saturday to take Marie on a two-hour library tour of all the libraries in a ten kilometre radius in their drafty olive green 1989 Renault 5, in order to provide for her daughter's intellectual cravings.

Books and magazines were Marie's best friends at that time, though not her only ones. She did also have two girlfriends, Nadia and Corinne, with whom she could share her impressions of the latest episode of Dawson's Creek, Beverly Hills 90210 or of the latest Backstreet Boys and Ricky Martin songs. But teenage-friendly popular culture was the limit of what she could share with her human friends. They would not have understood it, had she ever mentioned that she also indulged in Star Trek, Jane Eyre and Sherlock Holmes.

———

When MTV began airing Daria on French television, the show turned out to be a revelation for young Marie. She had instantly recognized a kindred spirit in the satirical cartoon girl and elected Daria at once her very own favourite heroine (all-media considered). Soon she had created her own imaginary interpretation of the misanthropic, nihilistic nerd girl in love with books and with travelling through history, fiction and around the world, even beyond it, into the stars. And rather than stooping to the intellectual level of most of her fellow pre-adolescent peers for acceptance and recognition, solitary Marie found great comfort in dreaming of being able to metaphorically kick all the mental Beavises and Buttheads around her into the ground with spite, spunk and spirit. Daria had helped Marie to better understand herself and, for that matter, everyone else.

The thing about television in the 1990s was that commercials were an integral part of televised entertainment. One knew that there was going to be a break every twenty or thirty minutes or so (at least on most public channels) and people didn't think twice about its usefulness – they went to the loo, fetched another drink or a snack in the fridge or (for the lucky ones) made out. Advertisements were generally accepted, on top of being largely unavoidable except if one zapped to another channel or turned off the television (hence taking the considerable risk of missing part of the programme if one tuned back in too late).

Especially during children's programmes, the profusion of toys, sweets and accessories that were punched through the screen and through the developing consumer's retina into their minds in twenty to thirty second intervals proved to be most effective. Children sooner or later ended up badgering their parents for one toy or the other – and sooner or later their parents would give in to the mass consumption doctrine, the high and mighty force at work.

Like many French children of her generation, Marie, too, watched the commercials with transported interest. Even more so since her mother could hardly ever afford to buy her any toys, plushies or dolls. But seeing them at Nadia's and Corinne's homes, her friends being slightly more fortunate than herself for simple and almost insignificant reasons – having two parents, for instance – made Marie resentful of her own situation and envious of her friends. She realized that she would never be able to walk enough dogs and shop for enough old ladies to be able to buy all the things she began to feel an increasingly urgent hunger for.

The first time she stole something was a celebrity tabloid. It had been a sort of means to test herself, to see if she had it in her. Her target didn't even have to be something interesting but might as well be, of course.

One afternoon during the summer break, she went to the grocery store at the bottom of the neighbouring building and leisurely browsed through the aisles. It was so hot the omnipresent concrete felt as though it was going to reach the boiling point any day. Children and teenagers wandering aimlessly through stores or shopping malls in search of some relief from the furnace were commonplace. When Marie had reached the newspaper and magazine aisle, she checked carefully, without wasting precious time, if the air was clear. Once she was sure, she stealthily slipped an issue of Closer Magazine into the back of her jeans hiding the rest of it under her t-shirt and walked out empty-handed.

No one had seen her take it and Marie was delighted about her first successful misdemeanour. Back in her room, she could still feel the tingle of exaltation in her stomach. For that feeling alone, she thought, it had already been worth the risk.

Although delinquent Marie didn't become an adrenaline junkie, she still went on stealing through the summer and the next few months until Christmas. Her being envious of her friends caused her to steal from them, too, a couple of times – a bangle and a lipstick. But on those occasions she had actually felt bad about what she had done. While she didn't want to ruin her friendships by confessing, Marie decided she would not do it again and rather focus on magazines instead. On particularly successful days she would nick a Glamour or Elle for Nadia and Corinne, too.

Her mother barely noticed the rather sudden profusion of celebrity and lifestyle magazines in her daughter's bedroom during the following months. Aline had too much on her plate already and was too exhausted most days after work to inquire about a bunch of magazines she assumed her daughter had bought with honestly earned money. She had no reason to believe otherwise.

On the first day of October, every year, the amount of toys, sweets, electronic devices and home gadgets of all sorts that were advertised on television, when Marie was still a child, increased drastically almost overnight. It was hard to tell exactly how there could be more commercials than the rest of the year with even more products on show, but to eleven-year-old Marie it certainly felt that way.

And then, on a Saturday morning in mid-December, there *she* was; wedged right in between two parts of an episode of one of her cherished Japanese animation series, along with seven minutes worth of even more magically delightful and oh so desirable toys: Business-Woman-And-Evening-Gown-In-One Barbie. During the day, she was a young, attractive and successful high class business woman in a smart perfecto-and-knee-long-skirt combo that magically turned into an extraordinary princess-style evening gown to go dining in a classy gastronomical restaurant and dancing with her boyfriend, Ken, after work.

There was nothing in the whole world that young Marie could have wanted more than to possess that doll. The commercial break ended and the anime show resumed at a crucial turning point in the plot – but Marie was not paying attention anymore. She had to have that doll. And she was sure that, although she knew that many things required a certain amount of patience in order to achieve fruition or satisfaction, her patience would run out very soon.

She decided to go into town that day, took the train into Paris and the Metro until she reached the huge and famous Paris department store. Any larger supermarket would have done; there was a Toys R Us much closer to her home. But Marie wanted to avoid being seen by anyone who could have recognized and denounced her to her mother. So it seemed to be a very reasonable choice to put as much distance between where she lived and the crime-scene-to-be.

The entire excursion had taken her several hours. Marie arrived back home with just enough time to bask in the joy of having achieved what she had set her mind to and – much more importantly – the joy of possessing the doll from the commercial. Aline arrived half an hour later and all along that Saturday's library tour found that her daughter was in a particularly good mood.

Every day until the Christmas holidays, Marie beamed with the sheer joy of knowing that she had her wonderful doll waiting for her in her room. Of course she had to play with it in secret since a brand new expensive doll would doubtlessly have aroused her mother's suspicion. But Marie was cautious.

On the last Sunday before Christmas, Aline had invited Maurine over for lunch. Much to Marie's surprise, Maurine had brought a Christmas present for her. Marie didn't know Maurine well enough to be able to say she liked her, but she sensed something, even though it was just a feeling, that made her feel comfortable with their neighbour.

The girl had thought on occasion that they did both have the same raven black hair. There also was something about the oval shape of Maurine's face, and about her thin lips that somehow reminded Marie of her own. She considered Maurine to be neither pretty nor unpleasant to look at but plain, and judged that she was of medium height with a rather shapely stature and what Marie decided was a decently sized bosom and not quite flat buttocks. Maurine's brown eyes had a depth Marie had never noticed in anyone else before, except maybe, possibly, in her own. And she had an aura about her of someone Marie was sure she knew, but for the hell of it could not figure out from where or when – like a permanent yet untraceable déjà-vu.

Marie quite naturally thanked Maurine politely for her present and asked if she could open it right away, Christmas being still a couple of days away. Maurine having no objection, the youngster eagerly proceeded to unwrap her present.

Never had Marie known a greater disappointment than when she had removed the wrapping. In her lap she held the same doll she had stolen the week before.

PART 2

Just as Marie was showing out Mrs Aliagas, her floor-neighbours stepped out of the lift. She correctly deduced from the pile of books the little girl was hugging that they were returning from their weekly library raid. The girl liked to read.

The four of them greeted each other, inquiring briefly if everything was well and within a couple of minutes the exchange had covered everyone's state of health, school, work and the weather before the mother and daughter disappeared into their flat with a promise to talk more soon. Meanwhile, the elderly lady made it slowly and persistently into the lift. At her age, Marie had decided a long time ago, one had a right to take one's time and Marie always saw Mrs Aliagas to the lift and remained on the landing until she heard the elderly lady close the door to her flat, just below her own. It was a Saturday afternoon ritual for Mrs Aliagas to have Marie read from the cards to her.

Marie had always had some doubts about the validity of what she told people from the cards and the importance they attached to her prophecies. Although she was quite certain about her ability to read tarot cards and understand their meaning for herself, in a sense, privately – it was her neighbours' hopes and emotions that made it into a mitigated experience for her. She didn't think much of it as telling someone's fortune as she considered herself to be providing a public service, because she could, by dispensing a small measure of comfort to the people around her – a little light of meaning in the vast, frightening darkness of uncertainty.

The news that Marie was a card reader had spread like wildfire around the residents of her building and, in fact, of the entire neighbourhood when the subject had come up during a neighbourly conversation. Even her next-door neighbour, Lina, had become one of her clients.

Since the forty-something-year-old mother had helped Marie move in and solve some starting problems involving an unreliable heating system with the social housing administration, the two women had become friends.

Although Marie and Lina both had exhausting weeks – she, being a social worker for student counselling in several schools each week and Lina, being a single-mum and a hairdresser – they got to know each other better and eventually got together for a chat and coffee. They even went to a music festival in the summer now and then or to the Christmas market. Marie often worried about Lina and her little daughter, Maurine, remembering her own childhood with a single parent and how difficult life could be when you were only a family of two.

But remembering was a delicate matter, she had realized; as when her clients talked to her. How often did it happen that a person told her about events – even from a recent, almost immediate past – that had been unwittingly deformed by the teller; not on purpose but because of people's inability to recall certain details, thereby altering the nature of recalled events.

From a radio podcast about mental illness and memory loss, Marie had learned that, over time, the brain autonomously decided to store memories of memories, copies really, rather than to call up the initial memory of an event. And each time an event was recalled, it was actually the copy of the previous time the event had been remembered. And each time, the previous memory underwent slight, minute alterations in the process of remembering. To Marie this could only mean that the more one remembered something, the more the first memory of an event became over-written, as if one were driving away from a fixed point looking at it in the rear mirror until it left one's sight completely and what remained was merely the idea of what had left one's sight. After that podcast, Marie had found herself wondering whether she remembered actual events of her past or if she remembered a minutely altered copy of a previous memory.

She remembered distinctly that she had discovered her ability to read cards when one of her neighbours gave her a set of tarot cards when she was a pre-adolescent teenager. Ever since then, she had practised each card's significance, possible interpretation and the subsequent combinations. Marie remembered distinctly that, as a teenager, being able to call upon the cards to read events from the past, present or future had given her great comfort. It still did. But, now, some of her clients said she could predict the future, which she couldn't – no more than she could prevent it from happening. Marie had learned that it merely meant she could catch glimpses of what may still come or already happened. Cards didn't discriminate between past, present and future, they just stated – something.

She had also learned not to stretch that point since people were usually happy with even the slightest hint of certainty about their futures. They didn't need more uncertainty than they already had.

Mrs Aliagas's door clicked shut. The elderly woman had come to Marie seeking to know what the cards could tell about her son: Would he find a respectable young Greek wife while she was still alive? She had been worried about him not being married at forty-one. Marie had been able to tell her that he would marry; the Ace of Cups had come up quite early in its positive orientation, indicating a positive family event. However, she did not tell Mrs Aliagas that it was unlikely she would be pleased with her son's future bride. In fact, Marie suspected he was already together with the bride-to-be but had not yet told his mother. Out of principle, Marie never told her clients the negative readings, rather focussing their attention on the positive ones.

She went back inside, drew some cards from the deck for herself and laid them out on the coffee table while she sat down in her armchair. She pondered the implications of the combination she had uncovered for a while, sighed and put the deck back together into a fit-to-size engraved oblong wooden box upon which were added delicately traced permanent marker lines and curls and mysterious symbols. The box went into a drawer below the flat screen television which she then switched on to watch a quiz show until dinner time.

On the penultimate weekend before Christmas, a combination of time-worn materials and insufficient maintenance caused the main heating regulator valve for the entire building to blow out overnight. When the residents woke up that Saturday morning, it took some of them a moment to remember which season of the year it was – winter or summer. They found themselves emerging from their sleep with images of sunny beaches on their minds and thirsting for an ice-cooled drink. Unable to reduce the suffocating heat to a comfortable level on the thermostats, all residents opened the windows to let in the freezing air from outside and create a heat exchange with the doors opened on to the staircase. It felt like the height of August inside Marie's flat, ten days to Christmas.

Like most of her neighbours, she opened her door to get a sense of whether she was the only one having the same problem. It had happened before, she had heard from some of the older residents of the building.

When she got on the landing, Marie realized that the problem concerned all the people around her. Most of them were taking stock of the situation, talking to their next-door neighbours in their bathrobes, morning gowns or already in shorts and t-shirts. Some of them were happy about the heat but most were not. It was still a few minutes before sunrise.

The hotline at the housing administration head offices rang all morning. By 9 a.m., the answering machine was bursting with complaint messages. Naturally, the technician on the weekend shift would be dispatched as soon as they managed to get in touch with him. It was only a matter of hours.

Marie wasn't sure how the day would turn out but decided to take it easy. She tilted the kitchen window and went to the bathroom to brush her hair and teeth before she turned on the television to listen to the news broadcast in the background, while reading a magazine until it was time for breakfast.

During the morning, the staircase had been filled with the clatter of crockery, neighbourly chatter, blaring television programmes, music and the straining grunts of a young couple's blessed morning workout on one of the upper floors. At some point, after the couple had exhausted their mojo, Marie had heard her next-door neighbour's door shut. Since Lina usually left around 8:30 a.m., it must have been her daughter going out for a spell. Marie hoped that Maurine was dressed warmly enough against the cold. Despite the equatorial climate indoors, it was still sunny but doubtlessly freezing winter outside.

She thought of the fancy new doll she had seen on television and bought for Maurine, after submitting the idea to her mother. It was something, she thought, she would have enjoyed when she was a child and now she was happy being able to offer it to little Maurine; more so since she knew from the cards that it was very unlikely that anyone other than her mother would give her anything.

Once, shortly after they met for the first time, Marie had been curious about whether there would be any relatives to be expected to visit – perhaps a handsome brother of Lina's – but hadn't felt comfortable enough to ask directly. She had asked for the cards instead which revealed, rather sadly, that there wasn't anyone, not even the girl's father. When Marie came to realize, much later, that Lina never once mentioned any relatives, she felt all the more justified to give Maurine something nice for Christmas. In her opinion, children should have something nice for Christmas; they should be smothered in presents.

Then, on the last Sunday before Christmas, Marie was invited to lunch at Lina and Maurine's place. She had brought the present with her to put under the small plastic Christmas tree on top of the television. But when Maurine saw the gift-wrapped box, she pleaded with her mother that it would be cruel having to wait until the 25th of December to open it knowing that it would be there, waiting for her. Lina said that if it was alright for Marie she could open it right away.

Marie had been looking forward to this moment for the better part of a month. She was eager to see the expression on the child's face, hoping that she would be delighted. Marie was terribly excited when she handed the gift to Maurine – and dumbstruck by the brutal contrast between her own anticipation and the girl's reaction when the gift wrap revealed what it was. Instead of leaping with joy, the girl's previous excitement broke in on itself, like a sandcastle in the tide. Her smile fell apart, becoming a distorted mask of sorrow and disappointment.

For one heartbroken moment no one spoke. Lina was just about to ask her daughter if there was something wrong, if she was alright, but before she could speak Maurine's face almost mechanically switched back to a happy smile. She hugged Marie diligently and forced herself to laugh in an attempt to suppress her urge to cry. Marie had a feeling that Maurine was lying when she said that she was so surprised at first, and so overjoyed, that she didn't know what to say.

While Marie had a great time with her neighbours that Sunday afternoon, she noticed during their conversations that Maurine's laughter had become somewhat hollow and almost imperceptibly tainted with sadness. The doll she had brought for the girl had remained sealed in its box. It would have been impossible for her to know why Maurine was unhappy or that she already possessed that same doll.

Although Marie did not understand it, she sensed that Maurine's sadness resonated within her, somewhere deep inside. It was both a diffuse and parasitic sensation impossible to shake or point out precisely, but strong enough to make her aware that there was something wrong.

PART 3

Time stopped.

It did so because it was sufficiently self-aware to know that it had only a limited choice of things to do; apart from accelerating, slowing down, expanding and retracting, it sometimes stopped. It was perfectly free to do so, too, since there was no one around in the variety of universes who could tell Time what to do or when to do it. It did not have anything else to do either, for that matter. Time simply knew that it did certain things but never with any knowledge of its own motivations, or the way in which it went about them. It was also aware that it did not have exactly the same aspect in all regions of itself, that there was sometimes more or less of it.

There was no way of telling what Time would do next, although it knew (even though not why or how) that many have considered the implications of this undeniable, unavoidable and unforgiving circumstance throughout the aeons.

Then, something odd happened, which felt new – but Time wasn't quite sure whether it actually was new. It didn't really matter, either. Not knowing specifically what to do, or why or how to do it, Time began to fold in on itself, carrying in its wake the entire fabric of itself and the surrounding area; all the untold regions of itself with their myriad variations, moulding itself into another self-similar version of itself. The whole process was immeasurably fast and, when it was over, Time found itself to be almost exactly the way it had been before – only slightly different. It had the inexplicable feeling, somewhere deep down in its gut, that it was going to do it again.

PART 4

The building's main heating system had gone haywire late in the night of the second Friday before Christmas. Fortunately, rather than to cease functioning entirely and have everyone freeze stiff, the heating was running on its upper limit. While the outside temperature was just below zero, it was consistently thirty-five degrees Celsius inside the building.

On the following Saturday morning, most flats had their windows and doors open early to create a cooling draft between the outside and the staircase. The residents put up with the heat by dressing in shorts and t-shirts, tank tops, underwear or less, which made for a surrealistic scene in the middle of December.

Christmas was less than two weeks away.

Marie had woken up early, sweating uncomfortably and confused after a dream. By the time she got out of her bed and to the bathroom, around 6.30 a.m., she didn't remember anymore what it was about, but there remained the lingering impression of two diffuse shadows that could have been one cast by streetlight in a thick night fog, there, at the fringes of her consciousness.

She checked the thermostats of every heater, in disbelief, having almost absolute certainty that she did not raise the temperature before going to bed. Not that much, at any rate. Then, she dialled the number for the technical support of the social housing administration and got the answering machine. After considering whether or not she should leave a message, she decided against it and rang off. She thought of calling a neighbour but, after considering the time of day, decided against that, too. Marie didn't want to disturb anyone this early. She tilted the kitchen window ajar and went to the entrance.

On the landing, she realized that the heating problem appeared to be the same for all her neighbours. She could see some doors open when she leaned over the railing. Two neighbours a couple of floors down were already debating the situation in front of their respective flats. The door across from her was still closed but Marie suspected that Lina would be getting up soon. The hairdresser's where she worked opened at 9 a.m. and Lina always arrived there early. Marie left her door open, turned back inside and put on a pot of strong coffee.

About one and a half hours later, she was distractedly reading a cooking magazine in her pink fleece bathrobe while listening to the news on television when she heard Lina leave. From her armchair facing the television she could see across her hall and the landing to Lina's doorstep. Noticing the open door and Marie looking up from her reading, Lina called over to wish her a good morning.

"Do you know what's going on with the heating?" asked Lina.

"I tried to call the administration but there's just the answering machine," Marie said. "And Mrs Aliagas just told me she got through and said someone will be sent to fix it soon. Are the two of you alright, apart from that?"

"Yes, we're fine, thanks. I just need to get going. Maurine is watching television."

Right before she disappeared out of sight, Lina asked Marie if she could keep an eye on her daughter.

"I told her to come over to you, if there's anything."

"Of course," the reply came on cue. She always kept an eye on Maurine when she was at home, when it was possible, although she and Lina didn't always mention it explicitly. It was understood. Their exchange ended there since Lina had to be on her way. Marie drained the last bit of her second cup of coffee and put the cup down next to the ornamented wooden box on the coffee table and went back to reading the magazine.

When she heard a door shut and a keychain drop on the floor with a short-lived jingle, she knew it was Maurine. Marie peeked past the door frame, said, "Hello, Maurine. Everything alright?"

The girl was straining under the layers of her winter gear while she knelt to put on her shoes. She was obviously dressed for the cold with a burly blue winter coat, a chequered scarf wrapped around her neck and up to her chin. There was a pair of gloves and a red woollen hat next to her on the doormat. She looked up a little out of breath saying, "Hi, Marie. I'm alright, thanks. How are you?"

From her own doorstep, the woman noticed an air of excitement about the little girl.

"I'm well enough, thank you for asking. Mind if I ask what you are up to?"

"Just going into town," said the youngster while she straightened up again.

Maurine appeared to be all set, ready to leave. But something caught her attention as she began to sniff the air in front of her. There was something flavoursome around. Her neighbour must have carried the smell with her, the girl thought; it appeared to be emanating from Marie's kitchen. For one moment, it was all Maurine could think of. For one moment, she even forgot about the doll she had set her mind on getting.

"What is that?" she demanded a touch indignantly, as if such odours were unheard of, and before Marie could answer, she added with glee, "It smells delicious!"

Although Marie was quite confident in her skills as an amateur chef, she enjoyed a compliment when she got one, and smiled in half-humble half-proud appreciation.

"Oh that, that's just butter chicken simmering on the stove. I was planning on cooking some jasmine rice and making a little cucumber raita on the side," she said matter-of-factly to Maurine's brightening face.

The girl was also becoming rather hot on the landing of the over-heated building. Marie had no intention of interfering with

Maurine's plans, so she offered to put some of the food aside, if she wanted to have some later. But Maurine was still standing there, in front of her flat, like an indecisive Esquimaux. The two women eyed each other impassively for a few seconds, in silence.

After a few seconds Marie felt that it was up to her to continue; send Maurine going or say the next best thing.

"But if you're not in too much of a hurry," she ventured, "I think it should be ready soon."

She saw that Maurine was hesitating, still breathing in the succulent, silky, spicy smell of hearty Indian comfort food, wavering.

"Or you can wait until you get back and there'll be a bowl ready for you."

Maurine had really just wanted to find out what was at the source of that gorgeous smell. So, when she peeled herself out of her winter gear, she was still convinced that she would have time to go into town to get the doll she so eagerly desired and be back home before her mother returned from work. But upon crossing Marie's threshold for the first time she had immediately felt at home. Maurine wanted to know what was in each pot and pan and what was in Marie's fridge; and she wanted to sit in the armchair to see if it was comfortable, and to know what television shows Marie liked to watch. When the youngster asked about the hand-sized wooden box on the coffee table, Marie said it was for cards and that she could show her later.

After lunch, she offered her young guest another glass of ice tea with lime and peppermint which the girl accepted happily. They talked like old friends – almost as if they had known each other their whole lives. Then, her glass still half full, Maurine was beginning to feel very satisfied from the delicious meal topped with ice cold drinks and cinnamon biscuits. She stretched her limbs which had become a little sore from sitting. She was still thinking of the doll, but just not with the same intensity anymore.

It occurred to Marie that the girl could want to follow her initial idea now and she led the conversation back to Maurine's reason for going out. But Maurine did not seem quite as excited about the subject as she had been two hours earlier. Marie's eyes followed the child as she rose from the table and walked around the small living-room, quietly investigating photographs, books mixed with DVDs on a shelf, magazines stacked around the television.

Something caught Maurine's attention, as if she had noticed something peculiar without realizing it right away while the thought had crept onto the front stage of her consciousness. She swayed back to the photographs.

They were mostly time-yellowed Polaroid colour cilchés, some in sepia, of young and older people, in front of a hut or cabin, standing by a horse cart, in a field or on a prairie, women laughing around some sort of improvised camping kitchen. There were varying groups of children, and a couple of photographs of what appeared to be an entire family clan; at a glance, she counted over twenty individuals. Some of the children were also in the first row of the family portraits along with youths, cousins, parents, aunts, uncles, grandparents and possibly great grandparents, Maurine decided. One of the older children was cuddling a new-born baby sister or brother. Next to them was a small dark-haired girl right there, in the middle, perhaps about Maurine's age, who bore an eerie air of familiarity.

She looked closer until her nose almost met with the glass and held her breath. Goose-bumps started crawling up her spine up to the nape of her neck. Had it not been for the faded sepia, the setting she had never seen or been to and what appeared to be traditional garments, she could have sworn this was a fresh picture of her. The resemblance was uncanny.

She was on the verge of saying something when it struck her that the possibility of this being the case was just unbelievable and she dismissed it. Caught by a sudden dizziness, she let herself drop into the armchair, her mind sunken in the first stages of a light trance. Marie decided to let her be for a while. She cleared the table, leaving the glasses and a saucer with the biscuits and left the room to give her some space.

When she returned a few minutes later, Maurine was still sitting in the armchair but Marie sensed that the child's aura had undergone a shift, from sleepy to inquisitive; she was staring intensely at the wooden box, as if she were trying to move it through psychokinesis, not daring to touch it.

And suddenly it moved. In her dozy, half-meditation Maurine's consciousness noticed Marie's hand around the box. Somehow, the box appeared to be realer, though, than the hand, as it took off smoothly, floating in mid-air through the room until it landed again, over on the table where Marie placed it in front of her. She sat down, opened the lid and waited. Maurine took a seat opposite her once more.

Then her host reached for the cards.

"Are those playing cards?" asked Maurine.

"In a sense, they can be," Marie answered without looking at them as she slowly, almost languidly, began to place one card at a time in an imaginary rectangle between her and the girl. All the while she kept her attention on Maurine taking in each card with its symbols.

"What would you like to be later?"

"You mean after school? I don't know yet. Maybe a veterinarian. Or a journalist."

"Uh-hum." Marie went on to the next line, still focussing her attention on Maurine. "So you want to help the small and helpless and inform those who need informing." It wasn't quite a question.

"Yes," the girl said crisply.

For a moment they were both silent. Marie finished the third line and went on with the same trance-like slowness to the last one. Her guest kept following each part of the process carefully – Marie's left hand slipping one card after the other from the deck in her right hand; the soft rasping of card after card against the table cloth; discovering each new picture.

"What's this one?" she wanted to know.

"The Justice."

"What's it for?"

After only the shortest pause, Marie ventured, "Have you ever thought of becoming a teacher?"

Maurine looked up at her, as if she had just been the object of a minor insult; not outraged but ostensibly hurt. While Maurine enjoyed learning, she disliked most of her teachers and said so.

"Well, I know what you mean, believe me. But then again, they're not all the same, are they? Sometimes there's one that's not so much like the other teachers, someone who makes the whole school experience more bearable, right?"

It was true, she thought, since she had a distinct soft spot for her History teacher, not a sentimental crush, not at all, but genuine sympathy and respect for him.

"I guess," she said guardedly.

"It certainly looks as if there's something like that in your cards."

The girl stared incredulously – her thick furrowed brows over her dark brown eyes translated how credible that was – at Marie.

With the faintest of bemused smiles, Marie laid down the next to last card in the rectangle. Maurine's expression changed when she saw the bare-boned figure with a skull head holding a scythe.

"Oh, don't worry," said Marie reassuringly. "It seems to me that you are confusing this card," she said, turning around the last card, "with this one."

A man was hanging from a tree by a rope on one leg with the other bent to form a triangle with the first. His hands were tied behind his back. Marie checked the girl's face, found her initial shock had been overruled by curiosity, and said, "Now, this is the Hanging Man." After a pause, she slid her finger back to the previous card. "But this one here," she continued, "this is the Reaper."

Maurine looked at each of the two cards, the hanging man and the skeleton.

she asked, "What's the difference? To me they both look creepy."

The woman nodded knowingly. "Well, this one, the Hung Man, is what happens to all of us, ultimately; death and demise, corruption, at least of the flesh but often of the spirit and the heart, too. But it can also mean elevation of the spirit, closeness to the heavens." Pointing to the card next to it, she said, "The Reaper, on the other hand, is different. He usually has a flower, a rose blooming somewhere near, or a wheat shaft, symbolizing rebirth, revolution and change."

The girl was drinking in every word. Marie smiled when she said, "Don't fear the Reaper."

Maurine spent the whole afternoon with Marie. Her motivation to go out hours before had faded to the merest shadow of that reason. By the time she got back over to her flat, to get ready for the library tour, Maurine had all but forgotten about the doll from the commercial. When she and her mother got back home, a maintenance technician had fixed the heating system. Even when Maurine saw her doll in the commercial later that day, although still tangible, the desire to have it had become really bearable.

On the last Sunday before Christmas, the following weekend, Marie had been invited over for lunch with her neighbours. She had brought a gift-wrapped box for Maurine with a big red glitter bow. When the girl was done unwrapping it, Marie sensed a sudden shift in her aura. For a few moments time seemed to stand still. Perhaps it did. And then Maurine's face began to glow with joy. At that moment, she was the happiest girl there ever was.

Amour in Paris

JASMINE TRITTEN

The Eiffel tower dominated the view of the majestic city of Paris. Lights sparkled like stars illuminating the conglomeration of architecture and sculptures. My eyes feasted on Utopia after arriving from Denmark to my dream city Paris where I planned to study French at the *Alliance Francaise*. I lived with a family as an "au-pair" girl, preparing meals and helping to take care of two young boys ages six and three.

At first, I felt like a tiny ant in a huge anthill. Everybody around me moved swiftly. People talked too fast for me to follow. The French words I practiced at school in Denmark for three years got stuck in my throat and sounded like babble to my unaccustomed ears. For survival in the big city, I had to use finger language.

The French people refused to speak English. They said, "You come to my country, you speak my language." So, for weeks tears welled up in my eyes and rolled down my cheeks in utter frustration.

Eventually everything clicked in my brain. I understood more what people said rather than speaking the language. After two months at the school, I noticed a certain student. Whenever I glanced at him his dark eyes followed me. They glowed like globs of onyx under thick, black hair. His skin glistened with a distinct bronze color. I became infatuated with him. Obviously, the admiration was mutual because he asked me out one day.

"What about a ride around town?" he said. *How can I say no to this great guy?* I thought. So, I answered, "Yes, I would like that."

Off we went in his small car. As I sat next to him the faint scent of his eau de cologne completely intoxicated me. Besides, his deep voice became music to my ears when he explained the history of Paris. I wondered, *is this what love feels like?*

Approaching the Eiffel Tower, I peered up the amazing structure but could not even see the top because it disappeared in the clouds. After parking his tiny vehicle, we walked on a path along the Seine River. Under a bridge he leaned over and kissed my cheek. I almost fainted.

On the next trip we shared our common interest in art at the Louvre. Afterwards we sat and watched people from the famous *Café De La Paix* on the *Place de l'Opera*. A tingling went through my body when I felt his arm around my shoulders. He treated me like royalty and called me "Queen of Snow." Probably because I looked Nordic with my blonde hair and blue eyes – a contrast to him.

Who gives you gooey, delicious dates in abundance? Only my "Man of the South" from his hometown in Tunisia. I kept visualizing meeting his wealthy parents one day in his country while exotic palm trees swayed in the sandy wind. Blissful illusion. I walked on clouds for months.

The hot romance ended abruptly one day, after I received a letter from Denmark. On the outside of the envelope, I recognized my mother's neat handwriting. *I knew something was wrong.* Carefully I opened the ominous letter and read the content. Every word on the stark page jumped out at me, striking like arrows through my body. By the time I finished reading the last word, I felt like a pincushion. My mother commanded,

"I want you to come home at once. I have a perfect education planned for you to become a medical laboratory technician. It was extremely difficult to get you in, but with your aunt's help I managed. The education will take three years and be incredibly good for you. I urge you to take the train back to Copenhagen immediately to begin. Love, Mom."

The handwritten page dropped out of my hand. My thoughts got fuzzy. I felt like somebody pulled a blanket over my head. How I hated my mother for being so controlling. In Europe at the time, we obeyed our parents. My dream of studying art in Paris and of being in love forever with this amazing guy from Tunisia shattered. Instead, I had to go back to Denmark to study chemistry, math, calculus, anatomy, all subjects I disliked with a passion. My mother still had control over me.

For the first time in my life, I had felt free, away from the clutches of my mother. *How can my dreams end with a letter from her? How is it possible for somebody to have that kind of control over my mind? I am eighteen now, old enough to think for myself. My father died when I was twelve, so I cannot ask him.*

The written words in my mother's letter got bigger each time I thought of them, until they consumed my mind. I had to follow my mother's orders. Her manipulation worked again. *She has controlled me all my life, told me what to do, what to wear, where to go. Nothing is any different now. Even countries apart, mother is still domineering, commanding me at her whim.*

As if in a trance I packed my suitcases. The spark of joy I felt in this wondrous place had suddenly disappeared. Instead, pain burned my insides. *How could I let mother control me again?* I succumbed because at the time I did not know what else to do.

After kissing Paris and my *Amour* goodbye, I swallowed a last sweet, gooey date as the train pulled away from *Gare du Nord* towards Copenhagen. My Love ran on the platform next to the train blowing kisses my way. From the open window I waved to him until my arm was tired and he became a blur in the distance.

Life changed drastically after I returned to Denmark. I forgave my mother right away. For three years I studied diligently and as soon as I finished my education, I left my country for America. My *Amour* sent me a box of dates from Tunisia, and I thought of him many times, but we never met again. However, the infatuation and love I experienced in Paris transformed me somehow. It gave me strength and hope of what to look for in the future. Like the saying goes, "It is better to have loved and lost than never to have loved at all."

Away to Provence

ANNETTE TOWLER

There is something in the way that your hands sweep across
my body
Conjuring an image of a place in Provence
The richness of your character captured by Cezanne in the
Consistent, reliable sweeps and swirls of the painter's brush
Depicting the Mountains in Provence

You touch me with the look of a wide-eyed child who has discovered the
 meaning
Of life, a life in the mountains away from all the bustle of the
city and
You hold my hand like a boy, an innocent who has discovered the
joy of
 being.

I close my eyes and we run together across the mountains and hills of
France
The eagles soaring across the sky, the sparrows chirping to tell us
that our
Life together is good, the best that nature can provide.

There is something in the way that your legs spring across the
covers to
Remind me of a time when I ran across the mountains of North
Carolina
Singing as I drop down the hills to the valley, consuming
pancakes,
bacon,
Eggs and hash browns to fill up the emptiness inside.

You touch me with the peace that is found in the hills and streams
of an
English countryside, the kind of land where children crave the
taste of a
Crumpet, with dollops of butter melting into the bread, you
Remind me of my home.

You fire me up with a positive energy that makes me want to run
to the
Shropshire Hills, just as splendid as Provence, and to clutch
your hand
Exploring the twists in the country lanes and the English streams,
Jumping over stiles, laughing at the cows, and admiring the
melancholy
Of the sheep, who beg for shearing.

By your side, we paint the canvas of a life together, with all the
 possibilities of mountains,
forests, lakes, and streams that cascade down into our simple
existence.
We travel together. We travel to Provence.

Climbing for Camille

SUZANNE KAMATA

My daughter and I are in Paris. Over lunch at the Café de Musee (*quiche lorraine* for thirteen-year-old Lilia, who sits across from me in her wheelchair, and beef bourguignon for me), I suggest that we visit the Rodin Museum, which was just around the corner.

As part of my effort to prepare Lilia for coming to Paris, I'd shown her several movies related to the city, including *Funny Girl, The Bells of Notre Dame, Marie Antoinette,* and the French film *Camille Claudel,* starring Gerard Depardieu as Auguste Rodin, and Isabelle Adjani as his young protégée, Camille.

Lilia shakes her head.

So much for all of that pre-trip preparation. I wonder if she's tired of sightseeing, or tired of art. I, for one, have never been to the Rodin Museum and my heart is set on going.

"Why not?" I ask her.

"Because of Camille," she signs.

Ah. Camille Claudel had mad skills as a sculptor, and for a while, Rodin had nurtured her talent and taught her a few things. He also made her his lover. But when he moved on to somebody else, Camille had gone a little bit crazy. Her family had her committed, and she spent the rest of her life in a mental hospital.

After watching this film, Lilia's sympathies are with Camille. She thinks that Rodin was a boor, and that he was cruel for making his models pose in painful contortions for hours on end. Lilia has a strong sense of social justice, which makes me proud. Maybe she has learned the right lesson after all.

During our flight, I'd read in a French magazine that a new film about Claudel was debuting—one starring Juliet Binoche as the artist—about a three-day period of her stay in the mental hospital. Though I'd thought briefly about taking Lilia to see it, now I knew it was a bad idea. It would just make her feel sad.

"Camille's works are in the museum, too," I tell Lilia now. "Don't you want to see *her* sculptures?"

She nods. *Good*. We're back on track.

We finish our meal and venture out onto the street. Once again, we evade the lines at the museum, and are admitted to a temporary exhibit of Rodin's work. At first Lilia is diffident, but she gradually becomes interested in the hands and heads and bodies, sometimes imitating the uncomfortable positions of the figures.

There were numerous interpretations in the gallery of the great French writer Victor Hugo—not only his head, with its full beard and wild mane, but also his naked body. Hugo did not actually pose in the nude for Rodin. In fact, he was already dead in 1889 when the sculptor received a commission from the Third Republic to create a monument to his idol. Rodin had initially been prompted to sculpt Hugo after critics, finding his work too realistic, had accused him of casting his brilliant *The Age of Bronze* from life. His supporter, the journalist Edmond Bazire, suggested that he create a portrait of a prominent figure such as Victor

Hugo, who would never consent to having his face cast, in order to lay suspicions to rest.

Lilia, too, finds the nudes overly realistic. "*Hazukashii*," she says, averting her eyes. *Embarrassing.*

We go out into the garden where many of Rodin's most famous works are on display, including *The Thinker*, which sits atop the sculptor's grave. There is a replica of this sculpture in front of the Kinokuniya Bookstore at the mall near our house in Japan. I've also seen a rendition at an art museum in Tokyo. Everyone in Japan, including my kids, knows this sculpture even if they don't know the artist's name.

Back in the day, a lot of people didn't know what to make of Rodin. The fashion at the time was to sculpt idealized images of the human body for decorative purposes. Rodin was more interested in portraying the body as it really was, in the belief that an observer could understand a subject's character through his or her gestures and expressions. He sometimes sculpted only part of a body, a hand, for example – and considered it finished.

"Is it broken?" Lilia asks me, gesturing to the headless "Walking Man."

"No, he didn't make a head to begin with," I tell her.

At the far end of the garden, we come across a fountain. Lilia wants to sketch, so I settle on a bench to watch and wait and reflect.

Before meeting Camille Claudel, Rodin and Rose Beuret, his off-and-on companion for fifty-three years, had a son, Auguste-Eugene Beuret, who was supposedly developmentally disabled. At least one biographer doubts this story, and suggests that it was invented to cover for Rodin's indifference toward his son. As far as I can tell, Rodin had very little to do with the boy. Back then, the prevailing notion was that domesticity and art did not go together. Although he managed to create some sculptures of mother and child, the baby's crying disturbed Rodin when he was working. Rose left him with her sister so she could tend to Rodin. Under the care of Aunt Therese, Auguste reportedly fell through a third-floor window when trying to grasp an escaped balloon and suffered a debilitating head injury. As Ruth Butler writes in her biography *Rodin: The Shape of Genius*, his aunt couldn't control the boy and he got into all kinds of trouble. Although he did well at school and had a talent for drawing, his cousin called him a *"vrai diable,"* and his aunt urged Rodin to threaten him with prison—a possibility in 19th century France, where children over the age of six could be imprisoned if their guardians "felt they were intractable." Maybe if Rodin and Rose had raised Auguste themselves he would have turned out differently. And who knows what would have happened to Rodin's career if he hadn't had Rose around to pose for paintings and keep his clay wet and buck up his spirits? He finally married her, two weeks before her death, in January of 1917. Rodin himself died the following November at the age of 77.

During one of their off periods, he left her at their home in Meudon, and moved into the first floor of the Hotel Biron. At the time, it was a veritable artist's colony, having housed such luminous tenants as writer Jean Cocteau, painter and paper cutter Henri Matisse, poet Rainer Maria Rilke, and dancer Isadora Duncan. The hotel is now part of the Rodin Museum. After we explore the garden, I push Lilia up the ramp of the yellow townhouse. A museum worker admits us, and we tour the first floor.

Living in Japan as I do, I'm particularly interested in the sculptures of Hanako, obviously a Japanese model with a geisha-style topknot. I later find out that Hanako was the stage name of Hisa Ota, an actress and dancer trained as a geisha, and that Rodin had planned to use her as a model for a bust of Beethoven, of all people. He modeled 58 sculptures of Hanako, and sketched her countless times, often drawing without looking at the paper, keeping his eyes on his subject.

Unfortunately, there are no sculptures by Camille Claudel on the first floor, and there's no elevator to the second floor. I gesture to the majestic winding marble staircase with its wrought iron railing and explain to Lilia.

"Shall we forget about it?" I try to convey that it's alright with me if we don't see every nook and cranny of the museum.

Lilia takes a long look at the steps that seem to go all the way to the sky. Then, with a look of resolve, she points up. "Ikkitai! I can do it!"

"Okay!" I figure it's best to check in with the staff before we haul the wheelchair up. I approach a guy behind the desk near the entrance.

"I know there's no elevator," I say, "but is it okay if we go up? She can climb a bit, and I'll help her."

He gives me a Gallic shrug. "*Oui*. Go ahead."

I position Lilia's wheelchair near the handrail at an angle, and help her stand. She grips the railing with one hand, I grab the other, and she begins to climb.

Perhaps inspired by Lilia's effort, the guy rushes from behind the desk and offers to carry her wheelchair to the top of the stairs.

"*Oui, merci!*" I'm happy to accept help whenever we need it. This museum is not completely accessible, and I am done with being a martyr.

We rise slowly, step-by-step, without taking a break. Even I'm a bit winded by the time we reach the top. Lilia, who has climbed all the way with her legs bent at the knees, sinks into her chair and signs, "I'm tired!"

"You did a great job! I'm proud of you!"

Finally, we find Camille's head wrapped in cloth, as sculpted by Rodin, which we both recognize from the movie. And there is *L'Âge Mûr*, in which a kneeling naked young woman reaches toward an old man who is in the embrace of an elderly woman. This sculpture was interpreted as being a depiction of Camille's yearning for Rodin. Her famous head of Rodin with its unruly bronze beard is also there, as is *The Waltz*. Camille worked on a smaller scale. No one ever accused her of taking casts of bodies. Like Rodin's, her works are full of emotion, but with more grace.

On the way back to our hotel, we stop at a chocolatier, Herve Chavin, to observe another kind of sculpting. The window is filled with Easter candy as exquisite as art—a large, filigreed chocolate egg, finely detailed rabbits, and chicks.

Once inside we're drawn to the glass case of perfectly formed macarons in many colors. Lilia and I had tried to make them ourselves a couple of weeks before, so we know how fussy they are —you have to beat the egg whites to just the right consistency, you have to bang the pan three times when it comes out of the oven, etc.—how difficult, and how delicious. We select a few flavors—raspberry, chocolate, the intriguing basil, and yuzu, a Japanese citrus fruit that is often floated in the bath in winter.

Back in our apartment, I heat water and pour it over flowers that I bought at a Japanese tea shop and tucked into my suitcase. I thought it would remind Lilia of the scene in *Marie Antoinette* when the princess serves her visiting brother peony tea from China. But Lilia doesn't like hot tea. She watches the petals unfurl, and bites into a macaron. Although I am a little disappointed that she has declined to take even a sip, I let it go and drink both cups myself.

My Brother, The Coelacanth, and I...and an Epic Run Through Paris

DAVID LANGE

They say the best place to begin a story is at the beginning. Adhering to this theory, I am compelled to take you back to the beginning—approximately 360 million years ago. This is the date of the earliest known fossil record for one of the key protagonists of my story. No, not him. The other one. The coelacanth! This imposing armored fish shared the seas with a litany of prehistoric "monsters," the likes of which have fueled the imaginations of countless children over the years. The last known fossil record of the coelacanth dates to around 80 million years ago. Like the mighty elasmosaurus, plesiosaur, and mosasaur, the coelacanth was thought to have disappeared around 65 million years ago, along with the dinosaurs. There was just one problem. It didn't. The amazing discovery of a living coelacanth was wonderfully described in one of my favorite childhood books—"Search for a Living Fossil: The Story of the Coelacanth." The book belonged to my older brother and he graciously lent it to me. We always shared books and news clippings about such extraordinary things within our "Adventure Club." The first living coelacanth was discovered on December 22, 1938. The natural question—what else that was thought to be extinct (or mythical) is still hiding out there in the world???

Fast forward. The year is 1977 and my brother and I, along with the rest of my family, are on our first-ever international holiday. It was a two-week vacation in France and Switzerland. We had visited the Louvre early in our stay in Paris. The Louvre was an incredibly impressive museum and the awesomeness of the collection was not lost on this 10-year-old boy. My brother had returned to the museum to spend some more time viewing the collections with a focus on his favorite historical period—classical Greece and Rome. While there, he spotted something which caught his eye . . . and an obsession began. He was nearly certain that, upon the side of a well-preserved ancient Grecian vase, the fish depicted was none other than our own beloved coelacanth! Could it be? Were the Greeks aware of the existence of the coelacanth several thousand years before Marjorie Courtenay-Latimer and Professor J.L.B. Smith??? Those Greeks were pretty smart people. After all, they brought us Socrates, Aristotle, Homer...and the gyro and souvlaki, too! If this theory could be proven, it would be a notable addition to the already fantastic story of the coelacanth. My brother did not own a camera. His little brother did. And thus I set the stage for the story which is to follow!

With the stage set, the curtain opens with the Lange family standing beneath the Eiffel Tower on a warm summer's day in Paris. It was our last day in France and my brother was clearly sensing a "now or never" opportunity was slipping away. He approached me with the rather unusual request to be the official photographer for his history making Greco-Coelacanth Expedition. Well now. I had my trusty Polaroid camera and what remained of the only four packs of eight exposure pack film that had to last me through the trip. This was a tall order, to be sure. My Polaroid camera had been a Christmas gift, just seven months before—it was my first camera. No, it wasn't one of those cool pop-zzzzzip cameras that shot out a developing photo. You pushed the shutter button, then grabbed a yellow tab and pulled the chemical-laden positive-negative strip from the camera, timed the exposure for 60 seconds, and then peeled the photo from the negative paper, after a lovely whiff of chemical goodness. My sister used to be my assistant, standing ever-ready with a small brown lunch sack for me to deposit the smelly chemical negative strip into. So, with the Matterhorn and spectacular Swiss landscapes (and goats!) in my future, I had to make a critical decision. I couldn't let my buddy down! I quickly signed up for the adventure. But there was a catch. It was nearing the time for the Louvre to close and we had no easy way of making the journey. My brother was convinced that it wasn't too far away but we'd have to run, all the same, to make sure that we didn't lose this fleeting opportunity. I should mention that my brother had been on the Cross-Country Track team in high school. For me, a long-distance run was anything beyond the distance it took me to get around a baseball diamond. My parents bid us adieu, probably wondering if they'd ever see either of their sons again, and we were off.

The run? It was not fun. I believe the distance was just shy of 3 miles. I was hurting but, with my brother's encouragement...and sincere praise, I kept it going, my camera in tow. I felt very proud when we finally arrived at the Louvre, only about 15 minutes before they closed the admissions. We quickly made our way toward the stairwell that led to the Grecian antiquities section. And...it was cordoned off...closed! It was closed! Nooooooo! Worse yet, my brother then got that crazy look in his eye. I knew it well. It was that crazy "don't care if I get arrested because I'm on a holy quest" look! I was a little bit panicked. I really didn't want to see my brother get arrested in a foreign country. But he was convinced that we could easily climb over the cordon rope and sneak down to the room with the pottery so that I could get the required photo evidence that would make us both famous. In a moment of sheer brilliance, I blurted out the words "ELECTRIC EYE!" Surely, the most famous art museum in the world had its exhibits protected by some form of advanced security system-- electric eyes! There were probably beams shooting out left and right, up and down, and all over the place! I managed to talk my brother off the ledge. Whew! I mean WHEW!!!! I was finally able to breathe again. We were both very disappointed. But, for my part, not half as disappointed as I would have been seeing my brother dragged off by a bunch of Parisian gendarmes. As for the coelacanth on the Grecian vase? We may never know. I suspect Indiana Jones is still looking for it.

While this all makes for a humorous tale, there is a larger and more philosophical side to this story that remains very meaningful to me. I suspect, for my brother, as well. The story of the coelacanth wasn't just about a whole scientific community being wrong about a scary looking old fish The coelacanth's tale is one of several notable discoveries that lend some credibility to the otherwise scoffed at field of cryptozoology (or the search to substantiate the existence of species thought to be mythical or extinct). Yes, that means the Loch Ness Monster and Bigfoot and other such creatures. I must admit, I was a huge Loch Ness Monster fan, as a child. I would have pursued this passion further but then I found out that purchasing a submarine with a monster-detecting sonar was a little bit outside of my budget. I did, however, in 1981, descend to the shoreline of Loch Ness to touch the cool waters of that special body of water. Our tour guide arranged a special stop—just for me! She also lent me several books on the Loch Ness Monster to read during our time in Scotland! So—if the coelacanth was alive, perhaps "science" missed the boat on some other creatures, as well. Dinosaurs in the Amazon jungle? Maybe. Yeti and Sasquatch? Very possibly. The Loch Ness Monster? What do you believe? At age 10, I believed enough in my brother's vision and a mysterious vase to run three miles, in July, through the streets of Paris. At the time, the mission may have seemed a failure. Today, I cherish the beautiful memory and therein lies the true success of that special day in Paris.

Deeper Colors

CAROLYN (C.S.) DONNELL

Gwen Martin had finally made it to Paris. One dream fulfilled. They said you could spend days in the Louvre and not see it all. No time to waste.

Gwen painted back in Vermont from the days at the orphanage with her mentor, Father Bernard, but, at present, with a couple of notable exceptions, found herself more frustrated than anything else. When Father Bernard passed away, he had left her a little money and a ticket to tour the great museums in England and France. She hoped that immersion in the centers of great art would help. Paris and the Louvre was her last stop. So far, the trip had been enjoyable, instructional, and even inspiring, but nothing had sparked that deep place in her heart that was missing—something. Until now.

The painting was named simply *Reflections*. By Geneviève de Périgueux. Donated by Gérard Dumont, 1857.

The vivid hues of the sapphire blue water caught Gwen's attention first. Autumn leaves transitioned from a gleaming gold to a deep red and changed color depending on the angle of the light. As Gwen shifted her position, the water shimmered, as if a breeze blew across it. She felt giddy and stepped closer to the painting. The air around her turned cold. In the painting she saw a young man in the background, sketched in shadows, stepping onto land from a small river barge. She recognized the location and the man. She knew who he was. But how? She had never been to France before and never heard of this place. What was the name? Périgueux?

The scene swirled around her. She felt herself falling ...

The winter of 1788 sent a frosty draft through the narrow attic window in the garret in Périgueux. Late autumn leaves swirled down the cobblestone road, caught up in a brief gust of icy wind. The bitter-cold air entered Geneviève's lungs, burning the lining. A red-stained cough gouged its way to the surface, the third time that morning the old paint rags had received the blood offering. Not much time left.

She pushed an errant lock of hair back with one hand as she jabbed a long paintbrush at the canvas with the other. A faded scarf tied back the longer tresses of her hair, but shorter strands waved rebelliously at any attempt at restraint. Sometimes she contemplated cutting them all off. An artist in Paris could get away with that. But here, in the more conservative town of Périgueux, even in 1788, she would be shunned for such a gesture, not that she hadn't been already. But that didn't matter anymore. Nothing mattered now, except finishing this painting.

"Merde! Why can't I capture that reflection?" She stared at the painting.

Autumn trees and storm clouds, images in a deep blue river. It was the water. It didn't move, it wasn't alive. She grabbed a wet rag and attacked the section, smearing what was already done, and started yet again. Another coughing spasm defeated further efforts at painting. Geneviève sank back in her chair. Her hand fell to her side and the paintbrush clattered to the floor. She would not survive another winter like the last, at least not in this place. If only she could have stayed at the cottage with Gérard.

She was eighteen years old in 1787 when cholera had ravaged much of her country. Survivors like her were left in a weakened state, susceptible to any other disease that came along. During the following winter, the coughing sickness had taken more lives and left others chronically ill. She was no exception. The frigid air had found a permanent home in her lungs.

The coughing and fever were good reasons to stay at home in bed that winter, but Geneviève's rent was overdue on the garret where she lived and she was hungry. There was nothing left for anything as luxurious as a doctor. Probably not much he could do anyway.

So she sat in her little booth on the lower side of the market and tried to sell her paintings while coughing into the paint rags.

Jean Gérard Dumont Comte de Montaigne was a nobleman who came to the market on Tuesdays. She had seen the tall, dark-haired young man in the market before, but tried not to notice. You couldn't be too careful with the nobility these days. They usually didn't come to this part of the market. At least the honest ones didn't. But today this one stopped at her booth and browsed casually through her canvases.

"Mademoiselle?" He picked up the largest canvas, a painting of one of the stone villas seen through open gates off Rue Limoge Anne. "My cousin lived here once. I used to visit the gardens as a child." He smiled, his brown eyes reflecting happy thoughts. "You have captured the wonderful light that always streamed into the garden."

"Thank you, monsieur." Geneviève answered quietly, swallowing a cough.

He pulled out his leather pouch and handed her 30 francs.

Geneviève stared at the coins. It was more than the average unskilled laborer's salary for a month. "Oh. Monsieur, no." She tried to give some of it back, but he ignored her outstretched hand. She accepted the money gratefully, curtsying with her eyes downcast, and slipped the coins into her apron pocket. As he turned to leave, she began to cough. The cough quickly increased to a spasm of hacking. She reached for a rag. Red joined the other colors on the fabric. She staggered, but before she could fall, the young man's arms surrounded her.

"Here, you need a doctor."

"No sir, no doctors." The 30 francs might pay for a brief visit, but she needed it for the landlord. And food.

"Nonsense." He half-carried her through an open gate that led to a series of upscale shops and residences. A doctor's sign hung over one of the doorways.

She tried to protest, but she was too weak. The doctor, who seemed to know Gérard, examined her. She heard the doctor say, "Only sunshine and lots of it."

Gérard had taken her away that day, down the river, south to a farm he owned.

Thoughts of that farm rose in her memory: the scent of apple blossoms in the spring, the silkiness of the curly-haired babies of the Angora goats that provided mohair for the farm's main business; the sunlight in the kitchen, golden even in late winter–a wonderful light to paint by. A handmade gazebo overlooked an herb and vegetable garden. Inside, hand-painted pottery bowls overflowing with fresh vegetables and fruits sat scattered over a hand-carved wooden table.

Gérard came and went; he had other properties to oversee. Geneviève would see him off at the village dock and meet him when he returned. With the sun's warmth, fresh food, herbs, and Gérard's love, she began to heal.

But when the leaves turned red and gold, he departed and didn't return. With no word from Gérard for several weeks, the farm manager, who had never approved of her presence at the farm, forced her out and put her on a boat back to Périgueux.

Geneviève leaned back and stared out the narrow garret window. Multilevel stone buildings stuffed with flats on all levels, from the floor above the shops up to attic garrets, spread out in all directions. She had painted Périgueux's rooftop views more than once. Sometimes she went to the cathedral where Père Michel allowed her to climb the tower that overlooked the town and sit and sketch.

Père Michel had been like a father ever since, as a baby, she had been found outside the back door of the cathedral. He had given her the name Geneviève, after the saint. No last name, parents unknown.

She had been placed in an orphanage and was expected to become a nurse or a teacher. She laughed at the thought. *Nothing very saintly or pious about me. Never has been.* Those roles never fit. Nothing had ever fit her, except painting. Art was the only thing she cared about, her only talent or desire.

Père Michel was an artist as well in his spare time, and had secretly sympathized with the girl's dilemmas. He was her first teacher and had found ways to assist her in her pursuit of the perfect painting.

The town looked different from the cathedral tower—narrow cobblestone streets bordered by tall buildings, covered by tiled roofs of varying colors. The cacophony of street vendors below muted to nonexistence from that height. Inside the cathedral hung a chandelier of red-hued gold with three tiers of tall candles, the first row in sets of three, the second in sets of two, the third one at a time. When lit, they illuminated a massive carved alabaster altar below. Nine stained-glass windows lined the interior of the chapel. Geneviève's favorite was the figure of Saint Fronto pointing up to a dragon. She liked to imagine the saint using dragon scales to cover the Romanesque spires on the cathedral roof. The blues, greens, and reds in the windows, rich jewel tones deeper than usual, had influenced her paintings for years.

Deeper colors. That was it! Geneviève came back to the present with a jolt. She lifted her paintbrush. *Make the blue of the water more intense at the front of the painting and less back toward the shore.* She loaded the wide, round brush with cobalt and purple and applied it to the wet canvas. She switched to a smaller straight-edged brush, dipped it in white and jabbed and then pulled slightly across the water. The white mixed with the blues, bringing energy to the landscape.

She worked feverishly. It was as if her arm was possessed by another being, guiding the strokes onto the canvas. Reflections appeared in the water. Final strokes with purple defined the silhouette of a figure on the riverbank—a shadow only. The last time she saw Gérard.

Another swipe of her hand across her forehead left paint smears of purple and blue on her face, matching the circles under her eyes. The painting was finished, complete, her goal achieved. Her cough worsened. She grabbed the rag. Streaks of red coupled with blue paint as she slumped against the wall.

Three days later, the door to the flat burst open. Gérard pushed his way past the two gendarmes who had been sent to clear the garret and ran to the window. Geneviève lay in the chair, her body leaning against the wall, the blood-filled rag in her lap. He fell to his knees.

"Genn," he whispered. "Forgive me. I didn't know." He buried his face in her skirt and moaned. The gendarmes tried to help him to his feet, but he shoved them away. They retreated to the hallway. A while later, Gérard took her lifeless body to Père Michel for a final blessing, and then, along with her canvases, to the farm. Gérard buried Geneviève under the apple tree she had loved so much.

"Mademoiselle?" Two strong arms stopped Gwen's descent to the museum floor.

Gwen Martin looked up into a pair of warm brown eyes. "Oui" was all she could manage.

The owner of the brown eyes laughed. "Je m'appelle Jérôme. Jérôme Dumont. Et vous?"

Gina stared at the young man.

"You are interested in the painting? Yes?"

"Ye-s-s." Gina stammered.

"Would you like to see more?"

"Oh, yes."

"Then come with me."

"Madame Martan?" The young guide pronounced her name 'Martan'.

"Yes?" Gwen turned. She smiled at the French pronunciation. She had kept her maiden name for artistic purposes. Jerry didn't mind.

"The Conservatory President is ready for the award presentations now. Would you please accompany me?"

On the podium sat a painting, full of New England fall colors, but deeper and richer than normal, so vivid you could swear you saw movement in the leaves and the reflections in the deep blue water. Gwendolyn Martin Dumont's signature style. A technique, she told admirers she picked up one day in Paris.

For Notre Dame

LINDA DICKMAN

Distant echo of a chant
sung in carefree days
in the High Sierras,
so very far from France.

Excited to know the names
the great cathedrals.
To be able to lift our voices
in the hills, to the gentle Prince.

Mes amis, que reste-t-il
À ce Dauphin si gentil?
Orléans, Beaugency,
Notre-Dame de Cléry,
Vendôme, Vendôme.

The enemy here not
the expected, but a careless
flick, or cigarette ash.

Ne lui laissant par mépris
Qu'Orléans, Beaugency,
Notre-Dame de Cléry,
Vendôme, Vendôme !

Indisputably, everything was not taken
the Virgin statue, spared in the crash
a witness ever faithful.
The choir, spreading their splintered song
the truehearted, staying together
for the Prince of Heaven.

Choirs rehearse
spread your song
beyond the walls
your chorus strong.

Répétition des choeurs
Diffusez votre chanson
Au-delà des murs
ton refrain fort.

Pain Vin Fromage

ELAINE GILMARTIN

Pain, vin, et fromage! became our rallying cry, but our journey was not a seamless one. Separated by geography with one daughter on the west coast, the other in London, amidst a pandemic, my daughters and I wanted to meet up somewhere new and exciting —Paris readily coming to mind. The announcement France would open to international travelers on June 9, 2021, was all we needed to hear!

My older daughter, Sarah, was tasked with the itinerary and was the one who discovered Pain Vin Fromage, a fondue restaurant on a quiet Paris side street. What could be better than warm bread, a good bottle of red wine—or two—and melty cheese? Nothing I know.

Sarah and I met at Heathrow Airport, separate flights conveniently landing half an hour apart. A quick hug followed by an Uber ride into the heart of London brought us to the flat of my younger daughter, Kate, on Pocock Street, where she awaited us with COVID tests pre-ordered due to the high demand.

Yes, to fly into the UK we needed proof of negative antigen tests, and similarly, France would require the same prior to entry on the 9th. Once completed, we sealed the test kits and put them in a drop box to be forgotten until the expected email response within the day.

Just steps from said drop box, my younger daughter stopped abruptly, her expression going from one of joviality to blatant panic. Watching this evolution unfold, Sarah's expression became one of consternation, demanding to know what was wrong.

Kate's eyes belied bad news as she confessed she had forgotten to include the necessary barcodes for scanning test results to the recipient.

Reality hit us all instantly. As travel was still mostly novel at this point in the pandemic, tests were expensive and not easy to come by, each costing about a hundred pounds. And we would need the results for our Paris train ride Wednesday morning.

Sarah admitted to me later she wanted to throttle her little sister but restrained the impulse. We all needed to be calm and clear-headed, and as we had a much-needed drink at a nearby pub, we mobilized our brain power. If we did not get tests ASAP, *Pain Vin Fromage* would be nothing more than a dream.

Okay, we found two appointments for that night, but they could not possibly accommodate a third. Ugh. Persistence prevailed, and we found one appointment at another location and grabbed it, necessitating a harried, sweaty run through the streets of London.

Tested for the second time that day, we were thoroughly exhausted, and a late dinner at the Moon Under Water in Leicester Square renewed our spirits if not our strength.

The morning of June 9th we rose early, and we rose with trepidation. An early train at 8 AM, *excusez-moi, a huit heures,* meant those results better be in! Rolling our suitcases along the London streets, each of us continually refreshing email on our respective phones, my older daughter doing so while balancing a coffee cup in her hand, my nerves were shot. Despite that, I kept smiling and offering empty reassurances as any good mom would do.

If the results did not come through, I thought I could possibly bluster my way through the immigration check, pretending to be the ignorant and hopeless American who just had to get her daughters to see Paris. Would they show mercy?

Entering the station and viewing the French border police at the gate dashed that idea immediately and rightly so. They were trying to contain a worldwide pandemic; we merely sought melty cheese.

"I'm negative!" Kate suddenly declared.

Within moments, my results came through, corroborating my belief it would be negative. I looked at my older daughter, scrolling through her phone, her anxiety palpable. She tossed out her empty coffee cup, her frustration evident.

Sarah is a planner. She works hard as an attorney, working long hours, and work seeps into her weekends, weeks blurring into the next as vacations are a rarity. And with the pandemic straining everyone's emotional well-being, families separated, and grappling with illness, this would be a much-needed reprieve. I wanted it for her more than for myself.

So standing there eyeing the French border police, the only barrier to passing through customs en route to the waiting train, I momentarily imagined creating a distraction and racing my daughters through, but cooler heads needn't prevail as she received her text alert that she was indeed negative.

"Allons-y!" I cried in triumph, my high school French briefly surfacing in my stressed brain. As we proudly showed our negative COVID status and passports, we ran to the waiting train with only twenty minutes to spare.

Giddy with relief as we crossed under the English Channel, we reviewed our itinerary for the next four days with great anticipation. We would begin with Sacre-Coeur Basilica, dinner at a restaurant in Montmartre, and a tour of the Louvre and Musee d'Orsay. A descent into the French Catacombs, strolling and shopping along the Champs-Elysées, and visiting l'Arc de Triomphe. A full day at the Palace of Versailles, and then our final night in Paris to be celebrated at Pain Vin Fromage. We accepted with some resignation that we could not enter the damaged Notre Dame, nor could we ascend to the top of the Eiffel Tower due to renovations, but we would still be able to stand in the presence of history in all its beauty.

Among the first of the international travelers, we were stunned by the outpouring of hospitality we were shown at each and every destination, every cafe and restaurant, as each Parisian voiced some variation of the hardship throughout the pandemic.

Dependent on tourism, shopping, entertainment, and first-rate restaurants, Paris was hit quite hard by the circumstances of the pandemic. Much unlike many American households, Parisians live in relatively small apartments with many of its residents employed in fields directly impacted by the shutdown. Working a remote position in the comfort of my two-floor home and expansive backyard for the past year and some months, I experienced empathy and guilt in equal measure; and yet, our hosts across the ocean could not have been more kind, more welcoming, and more pleased to embrace a life long since on hold.

My daughters in Montmartre

My daughters and I, in turn, embraced this return to the living. We walked miles, circling the damaged Notre Dame, still in awe of its beauty. We ate croissants and Croque-Monsieurs, and we drank good wine. We engaged with shop proprietors, and my fledgling efforts to converse in a language I hadn't used since high school met with kind patience and encouragement. We stood in the presence of the Mona Lisa with no crowds to battle, we were able to savor the works of Monet and Gauguin, and Van Gogh. We descended into the Catacombs of Paris, the three of us walking in lockstep through the subterranean tunnels with nary another tourist in sight, the skulls and bones of six million people bearing silent witness.

Then there was the sheer delight of the Palace of Versailles, its decadence in equal measure stunning in its opulence, off-putting in its ostentatious display of wealth. Walking the grounds provided spontaneous shows of water fountains synchronized with music, culminating in the night sky alive with fireworks.

Palace of Versailles

Once back in the heart of Paris, we had energy to spare. A curfew remained in place with police sweeping the streets at 11 PM to usher everyone home, but with recently loosened restrictions, the streets remained just as crowded at 10:59 PM. The three of us walked down to the Seine, a bottle of wine to share, to watch the lights of the Eiffel Tower.

Seated on a low brick wall, we savored the beautiful night, the Paris skyline glittering in stark contrast to the darkness. Occasional passersby would strike up conversations, forcing me to recall those long-dormant lessons given that both my daughters studied Spanish in high school. It did not escape me that most of these interactions involved young men trying to engage with my daughters. Two rather persistent ones began using their phones for translation, likely not impressed with my efforts to convey their questions, much to my relief.

With the 11 PM curfew rapidly approaching, I walked a bit to throw out our empty wine bottles and cups and was surprised when I returned moments later to see my older daughter seated alone scrolling through her phone. Glancing up at me, she calmly informed me Kate had walked off a bit with the guys to meet up with their friend who was fluent in both French and English.

Heart sinking, I peppered her with questions; *Whaddaya mean she went off with them? Which direction did they go? What was she thinking?!*

Not an alarmist by nature, I began to feel growing panic as my eyes scanned the crowds at the bank of the Seine, people happily milling about, laughing, talking excitedly, the French police still a distance away as they prepared to sweep the area for curfew. With minimal light from the glowing Eiffel Tower reflecting off the Seine, it would not be easy to find her as my fears she was already abducted began to fill my head.

I was prepared to go full Liam Neeson a la *Taken,* when suddenly she appeared at my side, pleased to show me pictures they took, and contacts shared once they had a qualified translator. So the two young men turned out to be harmless students, now Instagram followers of my daughter, not some nefarious members of a criminal enterprise. The relief I felt was palpable and right on cue, as the police began their evening ritual to clear the streets for curfew.

My momentary panic became fodder for my daughters' teasing as the three of us sat outdoors on a quiet Paris side street, a basket of bread, a bottle of wine, and a huge bubbly pot of melty cheese on the table in front of us. And as the kind wait staff tended to us on our final night in their beautiful city, it did not escape me the preciousness of this moment. That it would take a journey across an ocean to a magical destination to remind me of what I hold most dear, that sometimes we are called to step out of the mundane, the routine, to embrace what is closest to our hearts. And on my solo flight back to New York, I carried with me the joy that was *Pain, Vin, et Fromage*!

Paris: City of Light and Love

WENDY JONES NAKANISHI

It is said that, after a period of war and domestic strife in France, in a bid to restore his subjects' faith in public order, in the mid-seventeenth century King Louis XIV arranged for the Parisian police force to be quadrupled and more lights installed in the city and that Paris's nickname of *La Ville-Lumière* or "The City of Light" dates from this time. To prevent criminals dodging the police in dark alleys or streets, Parisians also were encouraged to light their own windows with lanterns or candles.

Paris's prominent role in the Age of Enlightenment that followed —when it was known throughout the world as a beacon for arts and sciences—reinforced and confirmed the symbolism of Paris as a "City of Light."

On first visiting the city in the early seventies when I was a teenager, I was aware of Paris's nickname but had no idea it was attributable to its being one of the first European cities to adopt street lighting as well as to its position in the eighteenth century as the centre of the intellectual ferment known as the Enlightenment. I simply marveled at its broad boulevards and plethora of monuments and attributed the city's title to the fact it was well lit at night. I especially liked how the Eiffel Tower and the Sacré-Cœur were both illuminated and how for me, as a tourist, provided ready reference points when I made my way on foot after dark around the city. I also admired Paris's iconic streetlights and the elaborate lamps adorning its bridges as well as the Art Nouveau entrances to the Paris metro.

Paris! A miracle of beauty and style.

On that first visit, I was part of a tour—a large group of American teenagers being shepherded around Europe. When we were taken to a restaurant in the Eiffel Tower, I somehow attracted the attention of a handsome French couple and their child. They beckoned me to their table, inviting me, in somewhat fractured English, to slip away with them to see the "real Paris." I appealed to my chaperone, but naturally the proposition was firmly quashed.

I returned to Paris, on graduating from Indiana University, when I was twenty-one. I had never heard of the British "gap year" but, in retrospect, I suppose that was what I was doing. I planned eventually to apply to a law school in the States but wanted a few adventures first. I thought perhaps I would never be so free again. I decided to go to Paris and work as an *au pair*.

I'd taken French in college and my ostensible aim was to become fluent. But, in fact, I was inspired by the example set by my English boyfriend's elder sister. She'd left a well-paid job at a large Manchester department store to spend a year in Zurich as an *au pair*, ending up falling in love with a Swiss abstract painter and marrying him.

I will call my English boyfriend "Max" and his sister, "Jane." I had met Max during a Junior Year Abroad spent in Lancaster, in the northwest corner of England. We visited his sister and brother-in-law in Switzerland several times, and I was deeply impressed by Jane's easy command of Swiss-German and envied her exotic life in cosmopolitan Zurich. I suppose, perhaps unconsciously, I was hoping for something similar for myself when I decided to become a French au pair, Max and I having ended our relationship shortly after I'd graduated from IU.

Soon after arriving in Paris, I got a position with a wealthy couple who lived with their two small children in a small village west of the city. Monsieur de C, employed as a pilot for Air France, was the son of a countess and, as his wife (from a far humbler background) pointed out to me several times, there is even an avenue in a historic part of Paris that bears their surname. Madame de C was once an air hostess, and that is how the two had met. The couple was pleasant and they both spoke excellent English. They had a delightful baby son, and even their three-year-old daughter, whom I thought spoiled, was mostly biddable.

My duties were light. I think I was hired as a status symbol. I certainly performed no useful function in the household. I had nearly nothing to do. I accompanied Madame de C on the expedition to the shops she made every morning: the daily ritual of 'faire les courses'. She'd buy everything fresh—baguettes at the bakery, meat at the butchers, fish at the fishmongers, and the best quality vegetables she could find at stalls in the market square—and I would help carry the purchases home. I occasionally was expected to take the baby boy out for a walk in his pram. I had to sweep the dining room floor after our elaborate lunches and dinners and take the tablecloth out into the garden to shake out the crumbs. Madame de C occasionally wanted me to listen as she launched into a recital of her mother-in-law's iniquities. It was true that her mother-in-law was formidable. The countess would turn up in exquisite Chanel suits marred by the occasional old food stains. I marveled at her complete self-confidence, how she was effortlessly superior, commanding our respect and admiration.

Madame de C was an excellent cook and, apart from breakfast, usually just consisting of large mugs of milky coffee, she generally made all our meals. Lunch and dinner often lasted several hours—especially after Monsieur de C (who had his own vineyards in the south of the country) decided the provincial little American in the house needed to be instructed in how to relish a good wine. When he wasn't away working, Monsieur de C would retire after each meal to the living room to slump into a large comfy armchair and chain-smoke and drink bottles of beer while he read crime novels. Meanwhile, Madame de C would take the children to her spacious bedroom for cuddles and naps.

The couple employed a pleasant Portuguese maid who came faithfully each day to do the real work: the laundry, ironing, dishwashing, vacuuming and dusting.

While the maid labored away, I lounged about. Light housekeeping, a sympathetic ear: that's a general description of the extent of my duties!

I was even provided a new scooter to get to the French classes held each weekday morning at an 'Alliance Française' in a neighboring town. The provision of such lessons was a condition of my employment, arranged through an agency in Paris. I was also given every Sunday off, and used to take an early train to Gare Saint-Lazare and spend hours visiting art galleries and museums.

All this might make it unreasonable if not inconceivable that I soon longed to leave. I was living in the lap of luxury: well-fed and well-treated if rather poorly paid. I knew I was very lucky. Most au pairs were required to do far, far more.

So why did I feel the urge to get away from the de C's home? For one thing, I felt I was too old. Most of the au pairs I met in the city or at French lessons–many hailing from Sweden and

Denmark–were in their teens and had come to Paris straight after finishing secondary school, intending to attend a university or begin a job after spending one or two years in France and becoming fluent in the language.

My situation was rather different. As an American university student, I'd become accustomed to complete freedom in my comings and goings. I found it irksome to inhabit what increasingly felt like a gilded cage: to be unable to do my own cooking, to be constrained as to visitors I might welcome to my tiny flat below the de C's house, to feel I couldn't stay up late and do as I pleased. Also, given my hosts' fluency in English, my French wasn't improving. It was awkward when they'd quarrel over a point of English grammar and ask me to arbitrate!

As I've said, Max and I had recently broken up. When he suddenly and unexpectedly appeared in Paris three months after I'd begun living there, our romance was reignited. We soon decided to rent a flat in St. Germain-en-laye, the town near the de C's village where I had my French lessons. We decided we could earn our living by teaching English.

I don't think the de C's were particularly sad—or perhaps even surprised—when I announced my plan to leave.

St. Germain-en-Laye, the western-most stop on the RER line from Paris, is now far wealthier and more exclusive than when my boyfriend and I found a cheap flat near its centre. I imagine any accommodation on offer there now would be far beyond what we were able to afford in the late seventies. Max managed to get a job at the local Berlitz school, and I taught school children, housewives and businessmen, sometimes walking to their homes, sometimes cycling to such nearby towns as L'Etang-la-Ville and Marley-le-Roi.

At first, we were deliriously happy. We'd become infatuated with each other again. For me, Paris had become the city of love as well as light. Fellow ex-pats would often drop by our cozy place for a cup of tea or a beer and a chat. I'd visit the market held twice a week nearby, in the old market square, to prepare delicious lunches for my boyfriend. We'd go out in the evenings with friends to bars and restaurants, occasionally attending concerts or going to films in Paris.

But gradually the dream became a nightmare. Max began to experience what, in retrospect, I can only describe as depressive episodes. Once, for example, I'd prepared an especially nice lunch for him. If memory serves, I had a bouquet of flowers on the table. There were steaks, a dish of spinach in a cheese sauce, roasted potatoes, and a big leafy salad. But Max returned home for his lunch break from Berlitz looking gloomy and said he wasn't hungry. He then retired to our front room and lay on the sofa, his face to the wall, and said not another word.

I recall fleeing from our flat on that occasion. I felt I just had to get away. I rushed instinctively towards the chateau just down the street—famed as the birthplace of Louis XIV—tears streaming down my face, wondering if life was worth living. I suddenly felt someone grip my arm, halting my flight. It was Monsieur de G, the kindly middle-aged Frenchman who was our landlord, who lived with his wife and child just a floor above us in the handsome block of flats on the Rue de la République. He looked anxious, asked if I was okay, and when I shook off his restraining hand, was polite enough not to be offended.

I thought it was bad enough that Max had become unpredictably moody. But even worse was to follow. He became a hoarder. As I've said, even in the seventies St. Germain-en-Laye was quite prosperous. Once a month its residents were invited to put their large items of "rubbish" out on the pavement for collection. Because it was a wealthy place, this meant that lovely items of furniture would suddenly appear on the pavements on that specified day. It seemed Max couldn't help himself. He kept returning home with chairs and tables and bookshelves, making our already rather small flat even smaller and more crowded. I protested. I cajoled, begging him to take the items back, but to no avail.

It was a relief when a friend, an English ex-pat, knowing I needed to return to the States to see my family, offered me a lift to London. I'd fly back to Chicago from Heathrow. I'd been in France for nearly a year. Max and I had lived in our flat in St. Germain for about eight months. As the friend and I drove off, I knew I would never be back. That is, I foresaw I would never live there again, although I hoped to return as a tourist. I knew my relationship with Max was over, this time for good.

I loved France. I admired how the French people had a habit of making life itself into a form of art. I was impressed by their style, how well they dressed well, how they loved beautiful meals and delicious wine, and how they relished the delights of civilized, informed conversation.

A few of my French students who'd become friends scolded me for socializing mainly with fellow English speakers and failing to take advantage of my chance to enter more fully into French life. In retrospect, I agree. It was a wasted opportunity. But at least I got a precious glimpse of France as lived in by the French. And despite my associating it with the collapse of my romance with Max, Paris will always be, for me, the city of light and love.

Return to Paris

EVA ZIMMERMAN

There is a small tree in the middle of the courtyard, a bench nearby. I sit on the bench, look up, wonder which windows surrounding the courtyard belong to the apartment where my mother, father and I once lived. I was two when we left Paris. My mother and father, born in Poland, arrived there from an American DP Camp in Germany in 1947. After a while, though reluctantly, they made the decision to leave. Europe held too many painful memories.

It was 1951, my parents and I embarked on an arduous journey across the ocean towards Australia. I did not return to Paris until many years later. Though I had left, Paris had not left me. As a child my imagination drew me back. I longed one day to visit the city where I was born. It was not the monuments and cathedrals, not the Eiffel Tower nor the Arc de Triomphe, though I was indeed awed by the pictures I saw. It was the thought of a city that had been home for the first two years of my life. Had circumstances been different I would have grown up in Paris. What would life have been like? I would have spoken another language. How would I be different from the way I am today, more shy, less shy, more outgoing, less outgoing? What would my future have been had I grown up in Paris instead of Melbourne, or New York?

Europe was much too far from Australia to even consider a visit. But because my family's origins were European, I felt a connection, a strong connection. I spent hours looking at old postcards my parents had brought with them, pictures of the narrow streets typical of Paris and the wide boulevards, pictures of people carrying shopping bags with baguettes poking out from the top. I stared at pictures of the pond at Tuileries Gardens where little children in sailor suits played with toy boats. How I envied those children. I wished I too was growing up in Paris. How I wished the city belonged to me as it did to them.

At fifteen my parents and I left Australia for America. Paris was now a much shorter plane flight away. My first visit at age nineteen felt grand and wonderful. I was a tourist in a city that did not disappoint, its beauty legendary and classic. Years later, my second trip felt even more meaningful. This time I was accompanied by my husband, almost as eager as I, it seemed, to visit the place where I was born.

Montparnasse is a well known neighborhood in Paris. Outdoor cafes dot the Boulevard. It is where famous artists and authors, Hemingway, Fitzgerald, Jean Paul Satre once congregated, sat together for hours at a time, sipping their espresso and discussing world affairs, all sorts of affairs. I had lived on 47 Rue de Montparnasse, a street right off the Boulevard.

We took the Metro, my husband and I. There it was the sign on the train station wall, Montparnasse. My heart skipped a beat. It was an ordinary day, an ordinary sign for the other riders who were getting off the train, but for me it was not an ordinary day at all, nor an ordinary sign.

I am not a Parisian, have no allegiance to France, but while sitting in that courtyard at 47 Rue de Montparnasse, surrounded by buildings that housed an apartment that once belonged to my parents and me, I felt I had somehow returned home, come full circle. There was something familiar about it. Was it simply because I had imagined it as I was growing up? Was it that I had thought about Paris so often and for so long? Was it the prodding of an unconscious childhood memory?

Three young people at the far end of the courtyard were talking, laughing. They were oblivious to the fact that two people, my husband and I, were sitting on a bench nearby, just sitting, looking about, immersed in thought. This was their home, these young people. It was not mine. Like the pond in the Tuileries gardens this place belonged to them, not to me.

I am an American, simply a tourist, like all tourists in Paris. But buried deep within is the city's spirit and energy absorbed while I was still very young. That is what we do when we are small. Vulnerable, and sharply attuned to the sights and sounds of our surroundings, we carry within us each vestige and vibration of the places and experiences that touch us. Those memories mold who we become. They call out to us in quiet moments. They stir us in mysterious ways. For me it was Paris.

Spin Cycle on the rue Mouffetard

GERALD EVERETT JONES

It was 2 a.m. I couldn't sleep, and all of my clothes were beginning to smell like ripened brie. I wanted to find a coin-op laundry where I wouldn't have to use a credit card, but in techno-savvy Paris, coins are so yesterday. Here I was lugging a stuffed pillow-case around town in the middle of the night, stopping in kiosks to thumb the near forgotten remnants of pre-Web phone directories, looking under "Laverie—Libre Service" in the commercial listings.

I finally found a place near Panthéon that used rechargeable cash cards or else somehow billed you through your cell phone. I wasn't about to use my phone. The card thing seemed safe, but the machine that vended the cards (accepting coins, bills, or credit cards) refused to march, as the French so colorfully describe their frustrations with all dysfunctional things electromechanical.

There was no attendant at this (or perhaps any) hour, an automated laundry being one of the first technological innovations to provide totally robotic service to the sweaty working classes, along with those storied nocturnal places that vend coffee and pieces of stale pastry through little windowed cabinets to insomniacs and cabbies.

There were no other customers in the launderette from whom I might cadge, and I would have been otherwise happy to be alone. A hand-scrawled note taped to the pay machine said to inquire at the corner tabac for a cash card. So I left my sack of stinky stuff on the folding table and trudged down the block to the store.

The diminutive proprietor looked up with disdain, if not disgust, from working his Sudoku puzzle. I think he read me as a tourist before I'd even opened my mouth. I therefore attempted accurate pronunciation in a respectful tone as I cleared my throat in what I presumed to be the Gallic manner and informed him quietly, *"L'appareil au laverie ne marche pas."*

He asked for my identity card, which seemed to me the height of cheeky gall. It's not like I was trying to cash a check or book a room. But who knows what subsection of the Napoleonic code applies to vagrants who skulk about the streets of Paris in the predawn hours pretending the need to cleanse the filthy rags on their scabrous backs?

With an abrupt gesture, he stopped me from pulling money from my pocket. Apparently following an accepted routine, he laid down his newspaper and pen, walked out from behind the counter, fastidiously buttoned up his cardigan, and led me back at a brisk walk until we faced the offending apparatus in the launderette.

At that point, he wordlessly thrust his open palm at me, and I obliged him by handing over a banknote. He then removed the taped notice from the machine and gave the vacant spot a powerful blow—*bam!*—with his little liver-spotted fist. He then inserted my bill, upon which the machine promptly vended a mag-stripe card and a handful of coins.

As I gratefully retrieved the card and my change, he actually nodded courteously and toddled back out the door, turning back briefly—and oddly, I thought—to repost the notice on the pay terminal.

I confess that in the fogginess of my consciousness at that hour, I had trouble processing what I'd just witnessed. The relief of finally holding the mag card in my hand turned to puzzlement as it dawned on me that a different message on the note—such as, *"Mettez un coup de poing ici avant de payer"* (Strike here once with fist before paying)—would have saved the fellow more than a few trips. This realization was all the more difficult to accept when I guessed that, as a devoted Sudoku addict, he undoubtedly had more than enough brainpower to figure this out for himself.

My first hypothesis was that the late-night shift bored him to tears, and the occasional round-trip routine to punch the pay machine increased his contact with the public and also gave him a chance to stretch his legs. But, nah. Closer to the truth, I remember thinking at the time, it was just plain French arrogance. Yes, the machine had a glitch, and hitting it did the trick. But surmising that he was proprietor of the launderette as well as the tabac, I cleverly concluded that he wouldn't risk letting his patrons abuse his equipment. Telling your patrons to thwack your gear freely was risky. A bodybuilder might strike it with enough force to cave it in beyond repair, or some blue-hair might knock it from the wall with a furious blow of her cane. He alone would know just where and how hard to pound the device so it would vend, and that was the reason he felt it necessary to post the note and to require his personal intervention in each instance.

Having congratulated myself on the superiority of my deductive powers, I went about loading one of the washing machines with almost all the vestments I currently owned. Just activating the wash cycle was another technical hurdle. There were no controls on the washing machine itself. Instead, a control panel on the wall near the pay machine had a slot for the mag card and a numeric keypad. Each washer or dryer displayed a large number code. A printed chart next to the panel showed a series of codes you had to key in to activate a particular type of wash cycle on a particular machine. Geek that I am, the challenge was trivial, but I did begin to wonder whether having coin slots on the washers might not make for a simpler and less annoying customer experience.

One of the key-press sequences triggered the automatic dispensing of soap within the washer, with a corresponding debit to the card, so immediately upon completing this last entry, my clothes started a fifteen-minute cycle of tumbling and sloshing.

I sat down and stared out through the storefront at the deserted city street, which still glistened from a light evening rain. I hadn't brought a book (didn't even own one at the time), and I didn't feel sleepy. So I grabbed a discarded newspaper I found on the floor. When I turned it over to the front page, the universe dealt me one of those blows between the eyes that pass for meaningful coincidence but feels like Someone Up There is pranking you and has a really wicked sense of humor besides.

The paper was two days old. The first shock was the masthead —*Loose Lips, a News Corp Publication*. So now they have a French edition. I wondered whether they translated the LA insiders' blogs or have a separate European staff of showbiz hacks and underpaid interns. But that wasn't the shocker. What grabbed me was the file photo and the chilling caption: "Monica LaMonica—*Elle A Disparu!*" Someone had obviously leaked the story that Monica had disappeared from Farnsworth's boat. Although there were plenty of clues that the grainy photos of her sunning on deck were of the lookalike doll and not the famously fleshy star, her zillions of fans evidently preferred to think she had forsaken her long-running soap opera for the love and lavish attentions of an eccentric yachtie. So when the doll went missing, the tabloids were more than prone to speculate that the star had met with foul play.

Here I must confess why I'm on the lam in Paris and why this little news item brought a twinge to my stomach. You see, it all started when I tried to make my would-be girlfriend Felicia jealous by dressing up a life-sized rubber doll to look like the real-life TV star Monica LaMonica. My job at the time was parking cars at The Wuthering Palms, a luxury hotel where Monica happened to be hiding out as a resident. So, naturally, after I took a few long detours in a borrowed Bentley convertible with the pseudo-Monica (aka the P.M.) at my side, the paparazzi drew the appropriate wrong conclusion. I didn't mind their accusing me of being the star's new boy-toy, but then when they confronted Monica for the expected denial—she surprised everyone (and especially me) by admitting to the affair. Then, far from being angry, she hired me to keep driving her rubber doppelgänger around town so she could safely shack up with her secret lover (a mayoral candidate) elsewhere. Long story cut blissfully short, this ruse worked for a while, but the only way out of it—which she and I eventually craved—was for her to retire from showbiz and fake her death. Then I and a crew of co-conspirators publicly buried her likeness at Forest Lawn cemetery.

To complicate matters, the LAPD got suspicious and dug up the doll. When the thing went unclaimed (as was prudent, all around), they held a public auction. And the successful bidder was none other than my old boss, Hugo Farnsworth, erstwhile manager of The Wuthering Palms, who'd always coveted the thing.

Hugo was happily hosting the P.M. on his yacht in St. Tropez when she/it/they went missing. And now you're up to date with the news story.

If any of the gossip peddlers were to inject the doll into the story, it would be to suspect a story manufactured by the Hollywood studio publicity machine as a coverup for kidnapping the real person, or worse.

On an inside page, the article had a picture of me with the highly realistic doll.

Uh-oh.

Perhaps I'm now a "person of interest" for other reasons.

Yes, the media will be playing it up as if something has happened to the real Monica. That's the hot news angle. But she's home and dry in the backwoods and probably not even bothering to put on makeup anymore. It's the theft of an expensive toy, nothing more. Isn't truth the best defense? Worst case, if it becomes necessary for Farnsworth or anyone else to refute a kidnapping story, we'll just have to blow the cover on the real Monica's whereabouts.

No, it wasn't the tabloid rumors but the actual theft of the doll that had me worried. Farnsworth's request for me to help him recover the doll had put me in a helluva spot, but why me? It's possible he thought I knew something about it—mostly because I had orchestrated her previous appearances and disappearances, except for this one. And, after him, I was closest to her. I'd arranged for her to meet every one of the significant-other carbon-based life forms in her world, including Hugo. I knew everyone who'd known her.

Did he suspect me? He knew I was no poker player, so in the first few minutes after our meeting on his yacht, surely he would have known I didn't do it. *He probably thinks I'd be able to guess who did. And that I have as much reason as he does to keep a low profile.*

But if he hadn't been the victim of the doll-napping, he'd be the first I'd suspect of stealing her. Of all the players in our little soap opera, Hugo was the only one who truly lusted after Pseudo

Monica. Oh, he could do an amateur job of pretending to steal her, perhaps for some kind of role-playing pleasure, but having done the deed, he'd have no reason to brag about it, much less profit from it. Who on earth would care?

I might not be the best judge of character, but I was pretty sure he hadn't stolen the thing *from* himself *for* himself. Which is not as silly as it sounds. The doll is a one-of-a kind collectible, expertly crafted in the image of a famous star, with a face molded from a genuine life mask that seems to have gone missing after the doll-maker completed the custom order.

Remember, Hugo (or his broker) had paid a pretty price for her at auction in Los Angeles after the cops disinterred her. He might have had her insured. If he'd been paranoid about people wanting to steal her, his instincts about getting her insured proved correct.

I thought I could rule out insurance fraud. Hugo didn't seem to need the money, didn't seem to care much about money at all. As long as he had her and that sleek little boat, he had the two things in the world he cherished most, along with his freedom to do what he bloody well liked with either of those possessions.

And then consider his demented rant about their having had words right before her disappearance. His telling of the story was too heart-rending not to be genuine, even if the inciting incident was totally delusional.

If they did have a disagreement (all in his mind, you understand), and were she flesh and blood, it wouldn't take a Hercule Poirot to guess what happened. *Zut alors!* Fearing divorce and scandal, the old bastard did away with her! Except that—valuable as the doll might be in the market of adult novelties—she has no life to take, no rights to defend. If Hugo were irrevocably angry with her or just downright bored or if he suspected her of cheating with some hopelessly desperate stevedore, he could simply dump her over the side—and quite legally! (Or, maybe not. Is she hazardous waste?

You can't throw so much as a plastic spoon off a cruise ship these days, much less a big doll made of silicone and steel.)

In fact, Hugo would no doubt regard ease of disposal as one more superior trait she'd have over a living wife—along with unflagging sexual readiness, exemplary personal hygiene through the occasional application of inexpensive household solvents, perpetual youth (without special diets, bloating, or weight gain)—capped off with those rarest of female virtues—long-suffering patience and the tireless ability to listen.

"Inspector, I admit, we sailed out to sea, and I shoved my lovely wife over the side."

Lt. Gaston Camembert, a veteran of the gendarmerie for more than thirty years who counted himself a contentedly married man, would scarcely approve. But he would understand. Such crimes of passion do happen, *tant pis.*

Now, this would be a different case: "Inspector, I admit, we sailed out to sea, and I sent my life-sized sex toy to the bottom."

Whatever the inspector's opinions about men of a certain age who covet their toys, Camembert would most certainly *not* understand. You might as well tell him you drove your shiny new Ferrari off the end of the dock!

"I am afraid I must cite you for unauthorized waste disposal at sea, monsieur."

So much less complicated than divorce—*n'est pas?*

Do you see my point? Hugo could not possibly have done this to himself. Given their solitary existence on the boat, he had the means and the opportunity, but where was his compelling motive? Self-disgust? Hardly! We're talking about Hugo Farnsworth, the man who got off on the taxidermy-treated pelt of his beloved deceased cat Lascivia. From what I knew of his former perversities, his taking up with the P.M. was, relatively speaking, a healthy return to normalcy in all but the most minor details, most of them having to do with the absence of his partner's body heat and other wet, stinky, and too-often unreliable human bodily functions.

There remained the questions of what Farnsworth expected me to do about her disappearance and what I could realistically hope to achieve on his behalf.

As I was mulling over the way forward, a real blue-hair stumbled into the laundry. She was shrouded in a trench coat several sizes too large and pulled two hand carts full of clothing. But as I watched her, ignoring my presence, she hoisted not clothes but armfuls of wet bed covers from the carts and proceeded to stuff all four dryers full. She must have laundered the bulky items herself but needed the high-capacity machines to get them dry. From this I concluded she was the proprietress of a small, tacky hotel, not unlike my current place of residence.

As she proceeded to load the fourth machine, I caught her attention and gestured the unfairness of her usurping all available resources. She gave me what by now was a familiar Gallic look of disdain, assessed me up and down, then hauled the load back out and curtly pointed to the empty chamber, as if to say, "Well, get on with it."

My wash load was done, so I grabbed it and hurried back to the dryer, thanking her all along the way. But as I punched the appropriate codes into the control panel, I got an error message saying my card needed to be recharged. She looked at me like I was an idiot, a deadbeat, or both.

I was afraid that in the time it would take me to make the trek back to the tabac, she could, and no doubt would repossess the dryer. I studied the pay machine as if reading the note for the first time. She studied me.

Rashly ignoring the note's directive, I inserted the card, struck the front of the pay machine firmly with my fist, inserted money, and retrieved the recharged card. As I turned away from the machine, smirking at having once more defied Parisian arrogance, I came face to face with a gendarme who seemed to appear out of nowhere.

"Carte d'identité," he demanded.

As I pulled my passport from my hip pocket, the lady glowered at me, a miscreant felon who thought nothing of ignoring signs, defying authority, and smashing private property.

I didn't question, protest, or resist as the flic kept my passport and led me away. I did wonder, however, whether I had miscalculated. Something in my gut told me that the little shop owner, far from being the arrogant frog I'd imagined, had somehow judged me a suspicious character during our encounter and returned to his tabac to phone the police.

As I tossed the tabloid aside to follow the cop, I saw the Sudoku puzzle on the back page.

Excerpted from *Farnsworth's Revenge* (The Misadventures of Rollo Hemphill #3) © 2014 Gerald Everett Jones

# # #

Table in the Air

A COMEDY
REX MCGREGOR

SYNOPSIS:
Marie Curie prides herself in being a rational scientist. Unfortunately, her husband has fallen under the spell of a notorious "medium." To protect Pierre's reputation, Marie must expose the fraud.

CHARACTERS:
Female:
Marie Curie, 37, Polish scientist
Eusapia Palladino (Sapia), 51, Italian conjurer
Male:
Pierre Curie, 45, French scientist

SETTING:
Psychological Institute, Paris, France

TIME:
Evening, 1905

(MARIE and PIERRE are inspecting a small wooden table. There are three chairs around it.)

MARIE: It's very light.

PIERRE: But solid. No wires. We can rule out suspension.

MARIE: No air pump underneath. We can rule out blowing.

PIERRE: Marie!

MARIE: I can't believe you're taking this seriously.

PIERRE: You saw it with your own eyes. The table floated in mid-air!

MARIE: *Appeared* to.

PIERRE: All four legs were off the floor at the same time.

MARIE: Magnetism?

PIERRE: I came prepared. *(PIERRE takes a magnet from his pocket and tests the table.)* No trace of metal.

MARIE: Suction then.

PIERRE: Her hands barely rested on top.

MARIE: Enough to suck you in.

PIERRE: I'm keeping an open mind.

MARIE: You're risking your reputation as a scientist.

PIERRE: Gladly. To discover a force as yet unknown to science.

MARIE: Darling, she's been exposed as a fraud. Many times.

PIERRE: Inconclusively.

MARIE: She was caught slipping her foot out of her shoe. She cheats.

(SAPIA enters.)

SAPIA: *Certo!* I cheat. I cheat.

MARIE: You admit it?

SAPIA: *Ma sì.*

MARIE: There!

SAPIA: Sometimes I cheat. Only sometimes. I am—how you say?
—*pigra.*

PIERRE: Lazy?

SAPIA: Like a bird on the ground. You go near. It walks away.
Doesn't mean it can't fly. Flying is hard work. A séance is harder.

PIERRE: Oh dear. I was about to request an encore.

SAPIA: What you like to see?

PIERRE: You raise the table again.

SAPIA: *Uffa! Vabbè.* I do this for you.

PIERRE: How much?

SAPIA: You nice handsome gentleman. For you I do one lift free.

MARIE: Cheating included?

SAPIA: Not with nice polite gentleman.

PIERRE: Thank you, Signora Palladino.

SAPIA: *Prego.* Call me Sapia.

PIERRE: Sapia.

SAPIA: Was big crowd tonight. I not catch your name.

PIERRE: Don't you recognize us? From the papers.

SAPIA: I not read papers.

PIERRE: Really?

SAPIA: I not read.

PIERRE: Oh. We are Pierre and Marie Curie.

MARIE: Winners of the Nobel Prize for Physics.

SAPIA: What is this?

MARIE: Don't tell me you haven't heard of the Nobel Prize.

SAPIA: *Ma certo.* Big, big, big money. But what is this fizz thing?

PIERRE: In Italian, *fisica.*

SAPIA: What is this?

PIERRE: The study of how nature works.

MARIE: Including the law of gravity.

SAPIA: Ha! I laugh at this law. I break it every day.

PIERRE: Shall we begin?

SAPIA: Sit close to me, Pierre. Put your hand on my knees.

PIERRE: I'm not accustomed to touching a lady's legs.

SAPIA: *Insisto.* You must. To prove I not cheat.

PIERRE: May I suggest my wife...?

SAPIA: No, no, no. I like nice firm strong man grip.

MARIE: Go ahead, Pierre. For science.

(PIERRE puts a hand on SAPIA's knees.)

SAPIA: Nice and soft, no? A change from bony.

MARIE: Just get on with it.

SAPIA: *(Placing her hands flat on the table.)* Hands. Control.

(MARIE and PIERRE hold SAPIA's hands. SAPIA closes her eyes and appears to go into a trance, shaking violently.)

MARIE: Spare us the routine.

SAPIA: John! John! Flow through me!

(The table rises and hovers in the air.)

[To create the illusion, each actor puts the ball of their hands against the edge of the table, with their fingers outstretched. By pressing towards each other, they can easily lift a light table.]

(SAPIA returns the table to the floor and appears to recover from her trance.)

PIERRE: Amazing. The laws of physics must be rewritten!

SAPIA: Don't look at me. I can only write my name.

PIERRE: Leave it to us. We'll devote our lives to the phenomenon.

MARIE: Oh, joy.

PIERRE: We're twice blessed. First, radioactivity. Now... Sapi-activity!

SAPIA: Ah! You name for me. *Come dolce!*

MARIE: You'll win more than glory. A Nobel Prize.

SAPIA: *Che cosa?* Big, big, big money?

MARIE: Enough for you to retire in the lap of luxury.

SAPIA: How I claim this?

PIERRE: Er, there's no guarantee. A committee decides.

MARIE: Don't be a grump, darling. She's bound to win it.

PIERRE: Well, perhaps with our help, er...

SAPIA: You nice kind people. I split the Prize with you. Is allowed?

MARIE: Yes. Last time, a colleague received half the money for his discovery. Pierre and I shared the other half for our research.

SAPIA: Not fair! Should be three—how you say?—*uguali.*

PIERRE: Equal shares. You'd be willing?

SAPIA: *Ma sì!* One third of big, big, big money still big money.

MARIE: First things first. Kindly roll up your sleeves.

SAPIA: *Che cosa?*

MARIE: The clothes on your arms. Push them up, please.

SAPIA: What for?

MARIE: We must assure the committee there's no chicanery.

SAPIA: I not understand.

MARIE: Oh, I bet you do.

PIERRE: Marie!

MARIE: What possible reason could she have for not complying?

SAPIA: I am not custom show my naked arms to a gentleman.

MARIE: Pierre, would you mind leaving the room for a minute?

PIERRE: Look here—

MARIE: For science, darling.

PIERRE: One minute. Humor her, Sapia. Purely a formality, I'm sure.

(PIERRE exits. Pause.)

SAPIA: You think you so clever.

MARIE: You thought you were.

SAPIA: I have right to refuse insult.

MARIE: Feel free. Say you're sensitive about your chubby arms.

SAPIA: You posh people! Always look down on us peasants. You never have struggle to make a living.

MARIE: For your information, I was once a poor governess.

SAPIA: You live easy now.

MARIE: I have no laboratory. I work in a shed.

SAPIA: At least you have a steady job.

MARIE: At a university where women aren't permitted to teach.

SAPIA: You won a Nobel Prize!

MARIE: All thanks to Pierre. At first, only he and our colleague were nominated. The committee hadn't even considered a woman.

SAPIA: *Allora!* You struggle, too. You should feel for me.

MARIE: I do. I wish you'd find respectable employment.

SAPIA: This is all I know.

MARIE: You possess extraordinary skills. Become an honest conjurer.

SAPIA: Ha! You ever hear of a female magician? Name one.

MARIE: Eusapia Palladino.

SAPIA: The world accepts me as a medium. That's all it's ready for.

MARIE: I'm sorry. I wish there was something I could do.

SAPIA: Let me carry on as I am.

MARIE: Very well. You may keep your reputation. As a medium.

SAPIA: *Grazie.*

MARIE: As long as my husband keeps his. As a scientist!

SAPIA: We have a deal.

(PIERRE enters.)

PIERRE: What's the verdict?

MARIE: I saw nothing up her sleeve.

PIERRE: Excellent! Now, let's all work together.

SAPIA: No! Your wife did not trust. I can't work without trust.

PIERRE: Come now. I'm sure we can resolve matters.

SAPIA: Never! I will share the Prize with my spirit guide, John.

MARIE: I'm afraid spirits aren't eligible. Nominees must be living.

SAPIA: *Prejudizio!* I spit on your Prize. I fart on it!

(SAPIA exits.)

PIERRE: (*Sighing*) Such a lost opportunity.

MARIE: There'll be others. A company wants to make radioactive toothpaste. For a glowing smile.

End of play.

The Pace of Paris

VANESSA CARAVEO

Paris, oh lively modern Paris.
Fast-moving and exact,
mystical and nonsensical.
Artsy, vogue, flashy.

The magic of the Eiffel Tower.
A place to climb up solid iron
to the height for a perfect view.

The towering faith of Notre Dame.
Intimidating, inspiring, absolute.
Nostalgic in its precise designs.

And yet it is the streets, the markets,
the perfect crepe, the chic clothes,
the barely wearable but beautiful shoes.
The absurdity of the pace,
the chaos of shopping.

Meander past Belleville's murals.
Cross the Seine into the Latin Quarter

and explore and move and ponder.
Dream sweet dreams of romance
or chase a thrill in the catacombs.

Then the Louvre, oh my, the Louvre!
Drag the thoughts of the artists
out of works as old as bloodlines.
Embrace the ideals, the trends,
the moments in time captured,
wrapped up in delicate hues.

Paris is adventure, pure as can be.
It lives for the moment
and thrives on its past
in flashes of sincerity, like a fever dream
where hipsters and the Renaissance mingle,
in a chatty hotspot where hours fly by.

The Rose

SYLVIE BORDZUK

There was a young Frenchman in Nice
Took his wife for a drive on caprice
As they rounded a curve
What did he observe –
A red rose in the wall of a precipice

He stopped the car with a huge, startling jolt
Sprang out like a brazen, charged colt
Grabbed the bloom in his fist
And with a sharp tug and a twist
The perfect gift for his "chérie" did he hold

As he turned around clutching his prize
The scent of love lighting his eyes
He failed to perceive
A strong onrush of breeze
For the rose yet a second surprise

He dashed back to the car without delay
Saw us laughing and pointing his way
Peered downward and stared
At the stem – now almost bare
The aggrieved petals just sailing away

Dedicated to Gail and Serge, wherever you are

Travelogue – Paris, France, November, 1987

STEVE AND LUANN DEWOLFE

Shortly after Thanksgiving with our family in 1987, my wife and I went on a slightly-delayed 18th wedding anniversary trip to England that included a day trip to Paris. This travelog highlights the Paris portion.

We flew to London on one of the last flights of People Express Airlines shortly before its merger with Continental Airlines. The plan was to spend Day 2 in London visiting the British Museum, taking a day in Paris, and then spending a couple of days with friends and former colleagues of mine who lived east of London before returning home to New Jersey. It worked out well.

London in brief. When we arrived at the hotel in London, our room was not yet ready, so we sat for afternoon tea, with its small, crustless sandwiches, pastries, and, of course, tea. The setting was the hotel's sitting room with a well-lit fireplace and was already decorated for Christmas. This tea service was a first for me, and was both relaxing and enjoyable after the transatlantic flight. The next day was spent at the British Museum where we marveled at the Elgin Marble statues and were fascinated by the Rosetta Stone. We learned that the Stone actually had samples of more than one type of hieroglyphics and some ancient Greek, all with the same decree about Ptolemy, the latter thus providing the means of translating the first two. (Even though I couldn't understand what I saw, I couldn't say that it was all Greek to me.)

On to Paris, where we hoped to find some sterling silver at prices lower than in the U.S., have lunch at Maxim's, visit the Louvre to see the Mona Lisa, and see the Eiffel Tower before returning that night to London.

Our short flight to Paris was uneventful and too brief for me to try to remember some French I studied in school. We landed at Charles De Gaulle airport in a heavy mist that persisted all day and into the evening hours.

Our taxi driver hailed from Algiers and, frankly, was taking us on the "tourist" route until I asked the driver to stop the car and pointed out that we must be going the wrong way. The trip seemed to take longer than I had been told it should, and I was trying to see where we were on a map I had purchased at the airport. I fared better, so to speak, when I could periodically see the highest landmark, the Eiffel Tower, and we weren't getting any closer to it! The remainder of the ride was much quicker and - surprise! – the driver spoke quite good English and, in fact, talked constantly to "les Americains". He probably could have been quite a tour guide, but his service that day merited him only a minimum tip.

We had seen and liked a Christofle sterling silver pattern at Fortunoff's in New Jersey and had hoped to find a lower price for the tableware in Paris. Our taxi took us to a Boutique Christofle shop. Our experience was both enjoyable and disappointing, each for two reasons.

On the positive side, the proprietress and her assistant treated my wife and I royally. They appreciated and complimented my halting attempts at speaking French, with the proprietress telling me, "Ah, monsieur, if you could spend six months in Paris, you would learn more words and speak like a Frenchman." Sacré bleu! That made me feel great, but I came back to earth when my wife, who with her knowledge of how sterling silver was made, was also treated well in the shop, later asked me, "How do you say, 'what am I, chopped liver?' in French?" Oh, well.

Disappointments were two. Most of the patterns on display in the shop were startling to behold. The embossing, carving, and engraving were nothing short of fantastic. I could have employed a magnifying glass to fully appreciate the craftsmanship, but most patterns were very ornate, too much so for our taste. We were told that several patterns were designed and were popular for Middle Eastern customers. The second disappointment was the price of place settings. The French franc was trading at that time at approximately 5.6 francs to the US$. Even rounding down to FFR 5.00/$1.00, the prices of our desired sterling silver pattern unintentionally lived up to the French term for sterling silver, namely "argent massif": the price was as "massive' ' as that back home. We left Paris without it.

It was time for lunch, and we had made reservations at Maxim's. Interesting enough, the owner of what was originally a small bistro was named "Maxime." The restaurant was and is one of the most famous in Paris, and the sumptuous Art Nouveau décor of the walls and ceiling were carried to the tables and chairs. The six serving staff had slightly varied apparel depending on their function. I expected a very stiff and formal atmosphere, but from the maître d'hotel who welcomed us to the server who cleared the table between courses, the staff was uniformly pleasant and efficient and seemed to appear at just the right times. My wife had the venison, while I tried capon for the first time. She enjoyed the chosen wine, and our shared desserts, like the other dishes, were delicious. When speaking with the head waiter I mentioned that we were there for our anniversary, we were served with a small cake with a candle. As we prepared to depart, we were presented with a small china candy dish whose pattern matched our plates and cups. I've said that we were treated like royalty throughout our luncheon at Maxim's, but actually it was more like with joy and respect that they could be there for our special occasion. Wow! It was certainly not due to my attempts at French, although such attempts were clearly appreciated and gently corrected.

We strolled—yes, hand in hand—down the Champs Elysées toward the Arc du Triomphe and were somewhat surprised to see familiar names such as Abercrombie & Fitch, Banana Republic, and Adidas along with the expected French Guerlain, Lacoste, Gucci, and Dior shops. We only shopped the windows, as we wanted to get to the Louvre Museum. The mist had persisted, and the darkening afternoon sky was a marked background to the Christmas-themed lights and decorations in the shop windows along our path. On that boulevard, Paris certainly lived up to its moniker, the "City of Lights!"

The Louvre Museum was formerly a palace, and very formal it was. The steel, glass and diamond pyramid structure seen in present-day photographs and movies had been commissioned a few years earlier but was not yet in place when we were there. Despite the late season and the misty weather, it was clear that the Tuileries Gardens were nothing short of wonderful. My wife, quite the gardener herself, was able to point out a number of varieties of shrubs and flowers. The museum itself would be breathtaking if it was empty, but the collections of drawings, paintings, sculpture, etc. from several periods deserves far better treatment than I can provide. Seeing the pictures of the museum contents is awe-inspiring but nothing like seeing the real artifacts. We wish we could spend days there. The Mona Lisa seems to tell me something each time I see it, and my wife understands the background and processes better than I. We had seen the Mona Lisa and an imitation at opposite ends of a gallery in the Montclair Art Museum in NJ but couldn't get very close to the original. My wife has taken art history classes and wanted to see the painting again in the museum.

We rode past the Eiffel Tower on the way to the airport. The tower was lit up but was closed due to the fog and mist. Even so, seeing the lights on the lower section gradually fade as they climbed upward into the mist is a persistent image closing out our day in the city.

Traffic was slow getting to the airport, and the flight to London was delayed approximately 40 minutes due to the weather. We arrived after evening had turned into night. We taxied to our hotel where we greatly appreciated having a room service dinner—and breakfast the next morning.

We traveled east to spend a day and a half with a couple whose husband was a colleague from years ago and had become a friend; our wives hit it off well, and we have remained friends to this day.

All in all, a very enjoyable anniversary trip.

One takeaway: We had been warned that if you went to France and were not fluent in French, especially as Americans, we would be treated with disdain by the aloof natives. It helped that I could speak a little French with a reasonable accent, but either our experience was an exception to that rule, or perhaps the rule is not a hard and fast rule.

Another takeaway from writing this travelogue is that you should write down or record your experiences, good and bad, for travel and otherwise, shortly afterward and not wait for decades and try to remember all the details. It certainly helped that there were two of us on this trip. You can always update over time as memories pop up and/or your perspective changes.

I hope you enjoyed our memories of this trip.

Trickles in Paris

JASMINE TRITTEN

The city of Paris sizzled. An unexplainable energy took hold of one and transformed a person into another realm, especially a young eighteen-year-old Danish girl like me.

Home referred to my room on the seventh floor of an old apartment building in the 15th *arrondissement.* The Eiffel Tower gleamed in the distance when I peeked out the tiny window from my abode. On the third floor lived a couple from Tunisia with two young boys. As an *au-pair,* I helped the family with the children and cooked dinner for them. Each day I studied French, my favorite language, at *The Alliance Francaise.* Evenings were another matter.

After a delightful autumn party with my friend Birgit and several young male students from the Sorbonne University, I arrived "home" with a taxicab feeling good. Dressed in a long, coral-colored suede coat, topped with a tall, pointed beige hat, I looked fashionable. As I glanced at my watch it showed almost three o'clock in the morning. *So glad Mom is in Denmark and won't know what I'm doing,* I thought to myself.

When I stepped out of the taxi, I still tasted champagne in my mouth. The air felt cool and damp on my face. Under the bright streetlight, I searched in my leather handbag for the key to the building. Carefully I opened the heavy door to the front entrance. No lights inside. I gasped and stepped back. The foyer appeared pitch-black. *Oh my, this can't be true.*

Whenever I came in the door during the daytime, the old concierge with a scarf tied around her head, always welcomed me with, *"Bonjour Mademoiselle."* However, she did not work the night shifts when I needed her the most.

As I inched myself towards the old-fashioned elevator, my heart raced. Champagne still bubbled in my veins, easing some of the tension in my body. In my stiletto heels I wobbled across the tile floor, aiming at "the black hole." With force I opened the wrought iron door. After I stepped inside and pressed the top button for the seventh floor, I waited. *Please, please, please move,* I prayed.

Suddenly the old shaky lift ascended with slow speed. Until the sound of metal grating upon metal hit my ears. The elevator stopped. *Oh no.* I tried to get out, but the door would not open. Nothing happened even after I shook the handle several times. Trapped, I sank into my knees in the darkness. *What am I going to do?*

The Tunisian family had no idea I went out at night. They thought I studied in my room. If they found me in that awkward situation, I might not be able to stay with them. Therefore, I refrained from shouting, whistling, or making any kind of loud noise.

Instead, I searched the bottom of my handbag and discovered a box of matches. *Yahoo.* With trembling hands, I lit a match after another to find the door handle. I tampered with it again and again. The elevator finally moved a couple of inches, then stopped. Sobering blackness engulfed me. For a few moments I closed my eyes and clasped my hands in prayer. *Please God help me.*

With my fingertips, I kept juggling the door, but nothing happened. I gritted my teeth. *This can't be true.* My fingers started to hurt, and my stomach ached. From drinking champagne all evening I got a terrible urge to relieve myself. Quickly, I crossed my legs. For about ten minutes I wiggled and danced in the dark elevator until I lost the battle and my kidneys overflowed. Down the inside of my nylon stockings trickled a warm liquid into my fancy, high-heeled shoes. When I shuffled my feet, I heard a squishy sound, like the stomping of grapes to make wine. A minute later an unpleasant odor reached my nostrils. With lips tightened I squeezed my eyes shut. My heartbeat thrashed in my ears. *What now? This has got to be the most embarrassing and unspeakable moment of my life.*

Both of my shoulders tightened. I held back a scream realizing I had to get out of the sticky situation by myself. If anyone tried to rescue me, I would be mortified. *Calm down and think straight,* I kept telling myself and prayed for a miracle.

Only a few matches remained. I shook my head, pinched my lips together and kept working on the door. Then finally, when I pressed the top button again, the lift vibrated and moved upward with a clattering sound. *Hallelujah.* Except this time the "iron cage" stopped about two feet below the floor of my room. Another challenge to overcome.

Full of determination, with strength from I do not know except maybe my Viking spirit, I managed to slide the door open. *Hurrah.* By using my elbows, I pulled my body up onto the wooden surface and climbed out of the metal box. For the last distance to my room, I crawled on my hands and knees in the dark, leaving wet patches behind. After opening the door, I tore off my fancy soiled clothes, washed off, and crashed on the bed with a deep sigh. *Thank you, thank you,* I repeated over and over.

Except, falling asleep seemed hopeless. Restless, my thoughts kept going to the puddle in the elevator. Also, I worried about the damp spots leading to my room. So, when the sun rose before anybody got up, I tiptoed down the stairs with a towel and cleaned up every trickle. Then I took in a deep breath and continued my day as if nothing had happened. *If they only knew.* Thankfully, no one knew but me and I swore never to tell a soul.

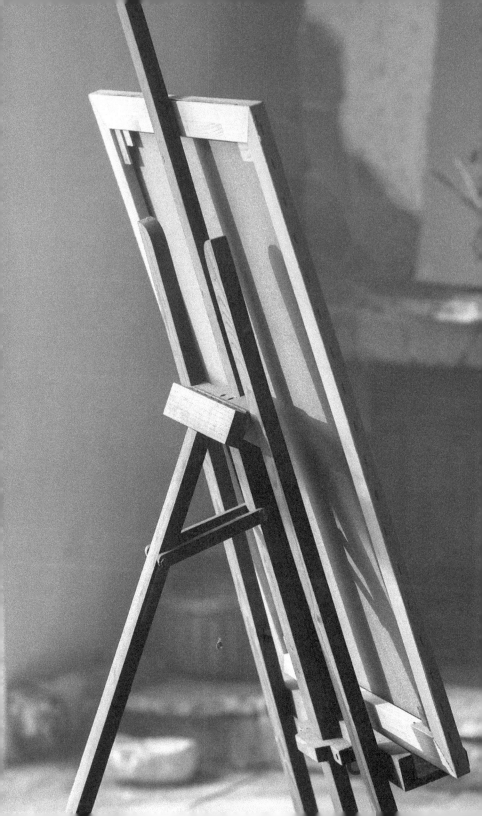

Woman, Blossoming

SUZANNE KAMATA

"Thank you honorable guests for coming here on this day when you are surely very busy, to pay homage to the great Taizo Saijo who was born in this very prefecture..."

Yoshiko Saijo stands off to the side listening to the curator drone. In her pigeon-grey kimono, with her hair pulled into a tight ball, she looks the picture of propriety. The artist's widow. The dignified dowager.

"...works gathered from collections in Europe and Japan, some never publicly exhibited until this day..."

Yoshiko looks out at the gathering. She sees wrinkled men in berets, one with long white hair. Another leans on a cane. One or two seem a bit familiar. Had she known them in Paris? That was so long ago.

"And now, would you kindly do the honors?"

All eyes turn to Yoshiko. The curator holds a pair of scissors in his white-gloved hands, a red ribbon festooning the handle.

Yoshiko reaches out with both hands. She takes the scissors, bows and snips the tape. "Dozo," she says, gesturing to the gallery where her late husband's paintings are hung.

The guests flow toward the first painting, completed when Taizo was still a student. It is of a field—a Japanese field, perhaps, not unlike the one near the house where Yoshiko had grown up. The one where she had started her career.

"Yoshiko!"

Yoshiko hunched down lower, her back scraping against a tree trunk. She knew that she was supposed to be at home, washing the rice for supper and helping to keep track of her five younger brothers and sisters, but she wanted to finish this drawing. Just that rambling fence...

She got so lost in her sketch that she didn't see her mother until she was standing over her. Her shadow fell across the page and then the sketchbook was snatched out of her hands.

"Lazy girl! There are mouths to be fed and clothes to be scrubbed and here you are making pictures!"

Yoshiko held her breath, bracing herself for the rip and crumple of paper. She'd spent hours on it. This was her best one yet.

But her mother didn't tear up the drawing. Not this time. She gave it a long hard look—the sweet potato field, the plough, the houses crowded together in the distance—and grunted. Then she slammed the book shut and yanked her daughter by the elbow till she was standing.

Yoshiko followed her home.

Later that evening when the dishes were washed and the youngest children tucked into their futons, her father called out to her.

"Yes, Otosan?"

He sat by the brazier, smoking and drinking sake from a small pottery cup. He held Yoshiko's notebook open on his knees.

"Did you do this?" His voice was gruff, but his eyes were kind.

"Yes, father." Yoshiko lowered her gaze.

"Then I think we need to send you to school."

At the Tokyo Institute of Art, the halls were full of young men with Rembrandt beards and baggy clothes. They all looked as if they'd stepped out of a Dutch painting. Yoshiko didn't fit in. She wore a hakama and her hair hung in a neat braid down her back. She had no interest in painting dykes and tulips. She was partial to chrysanthemums.

In her first class, she was assigned a seat near the back. She could see all of the other students in their almost identical outfits There were only a few girls, quiet and shy like herself.

The professor passed out a number of prints by the artist Vermeer —a girl reading a letter.

"You will copy this," the professor said.

Yoshiko prepared her colors.

"This is old stuff," the young man next to her muttered, "Why not Monet? Why not Degas?"

Yoshiko stole a glimpse of the student. He had a sparse beard, like the others. His chin-length hair was disheveled. The sleeves of his white blouse were rolled up, revealing muscled forearms. Yoshiko noticed the blue veins popping out.

He was looking at her as if he expected an answer.

"Why not Mary Cassatt?" she asked with a smile.

Four years later they were together on a steamer bound for Europe.

"Paris is the center of the art world," gushed the young man, whose name was Taizo. "The Japanese art establishment is too conservative. Moribund. If we want to create something new and alive, we must be among progressive thinkers."

Already, as they sailed out of Yokohama, Taizo was scheming as to how he'd meet the great French artists. Yoshiko sat on the deck, gathering images in her sketchbook – the vultures at the Parsi Tower of Silence, the young boys selling ostrich feathers in Aden, the purple hills of Egypt. She made a study of camels and Bedouins spotted from the Suez Canal.

Finally in Paris, they settled into a cold water flat in the shadow of Sacre Coeur. Broke, and longing for rice and green tea, they subsisted on day-old bread and syrupy coffee. And they painted.

One afternoon, Taizo returned home from a visit to a café with another artist in tow. A Frenchman.

"This is Jean-Claude," Taizo said. "I've told him you would sit for him." Whiskey wafted on his breath.

Yoshiko bowed, unable to muster a smile.

The Frenchman caught her hand in his and brought it to his lips. She did not like the scratching of his whiskers on her skin.

"Enchanté, madame."

Yoshiko said nothing.

That evening over bowls of burnt stew, she exploded. "What about my art? When can I paint if I have to sit on a chair all day?"

176

Taizo scooped a mouthful of stew. His jaws worked on the tough meat, the cheapest at the market.

"It's just for one painting," he pleaded. "We are so poor right now. Later we will drink champagne and dance in the fountains. I'll buy you silk parasols and a new kimono. We'll have parties..."

He was floating away on his fantasies, but then he caught sight of his wife's grim mouth. "Please," he said, taking up her hands. "I beg of you. Just this once."

As the months went by, it seemed as if Yoshiko was modeling more and more, while Taizo was painting less and less. "The French are wild about Japan," he said. "Everyone's painting Japanese vases, fans, kimonos. And of course, they want to paint our women."

Taizo, on the other hand, wanted to paint les françaises. He stayed out till all hours drinking at the feet of the can-can girls, commiserating with compatriots, and then sleeping till noon.

Meanwhile, Yoshiko rose at dawn and began mixing colors. She stayed at her easel until Taizo stirred and then she hid her work under a sheet. He sipped his morning café before heading off to his studio, too bleary to notice the paint stains on his wife's hands.

And then one afternoon, around the time of day that Taizo was usually in his studio, he returned to find Yoshiko with a brush in her hand. She moved to block her easel and the beginnings of a garden. But Taizo didn't even seem to notice. He was holding a bottle of champagne—the expensive kind. His face was a deep red from drinking.

"Ma petite," he said, spinning into the room. "On va celebrer."

Yoshiko frowned at his atrocious accent. "What is there to celebrate?" she asked, rising, hands on hips. That bottle was worth three sittings for Jean-Claude, money better spent on meat and bread.

"I've sold a painting to the Countess. Maybe two or three."

The Countess was famous. Even Yoshiko, who never went to the cafes and cabarets, had heard of her. She was known not only for her exotic pets and scandalous liaisons (husbands, scoundrels, a woman or two), but also for her patronage of the arts. Rumor had it that she'd saved more than one poet from starvation and suicide. She was a trendsetter. If the Countess showed interest in an artist, others soon did, too.

Taizo started spending more time at home. He wanted to bring potential patrons around for authentic Japanese meals. The French interest in Japan went beyond art and Taizo was exploiting it for all it was worth.

Suddenly, Yoshiko was performing a tea ceremony twice a day. When she might have been working on her own art, she was sweeping out corners and packing rice balls in her palms.

But things were better. They could afford a new loaf of bread and cheese and fresh fruit every day. The meat in the pot was tender. They indulged in flaky tarts from the patisserie down the street.

That is, until the morning Taizo woke up coughing. Blood spattered the white sheets. Yoshiko lost herself for a moment in the crimson patterns before a new dawning caused her stomach to wrench.

"Tuberculosis," the bearded doctor said. Taizo was admitted to a ward for the contagious, a dark corner in an otherwise lively hospital.

When Yoshiko arrived each morning with a basket of oranges and rice balls, she held a handkerchief pressed to her nose and mouth. She kept it there for the length of the visit and didn't dare touch him.

In the afternoons, she went from gallery to gallery, selling his finished paintings. A few incomplete canvases were propped against the wall having been temporarily abandoned for commissioned portraits of daughters and lap dogs.

When Taizo returned home, he was only well enough to paint for an hour or two a day before collapsing in fatigue. Yoshiko helped him back into bed then sat at the table, head in hands, listening to the breath rattle in his chest. They were doomed, she thought. She would never be able to go back to Japan.

Snow swirled outside the window. She shivered and rose to make a pot of tea. Seeing a bottle of whiskey on the shelf, she changed her mind.

The first sip made her shudder. The second made her cough. By the third swallow, her limbs were beginning to heat up. Suddenly, the snow, her sleeping husband and the empty purse no longer seemed so severe.

And then she bent over the chamber pot and threw up.

As she huddled on the floor, dabbing at her brow, she caught sight of a landscape Taizo had left undone. The trees standing alone made her feel desolate. She would add human figures.

The next afternoon, while her husband snored, she brought out her easel and palette and began mixing color. Taizo had a particular technique, a fondness for gouache and thick impasto. She experimented on bits of cloth until she had a close approximation.

Finally, she turned to her husband's canvas, a brush poised in the air. Her heart galloped wildly. What if she ruined it? What if she couldn't sell it? She thought of the francs rattling in the coffee can. What if she could?

With a deep breath she began to work. As she became more and more engrossed, she forgot her violation. The pure joy of creation filled her. She didn't even notice when it stopped snowing.

By the time she finished, it was dark. Taizo was just waking up. He would need his supper. She set the canvas aside to dry and covered her easel with a worn sheet.

She let the finished painting sit there for a few days, a little afraid of what she was planning to do next. When the pantry was bare, but for a few rat droppings, and there was no longer enough money to pay the next month's rent, she took a deep breath and rolled up the canvas.

"Where are you going?" Taizo's weak voice rose from the bed.

"For a promenade," she said, and left before he could ask any more questions.

She walked along the icy streets, trying to ignore the wind biting her face. Twice, she slipped and fell. By the time she arrived at the Countess's door, her fingers, though gloved, were stiff with cold. She stamped her feet to warm them and pressed the bell.

A maid appeared almost immediately. The white apron she wore over her black uniform was crisp and spotless. Yoshiko couldn't believe she did any housework at all. Maybe her job was simply answering the door.

"I'm here to show the Countess a painting," she said.

The maid nodded and motioned her inside.

As Yoshiko fumbled in her purse for a calling card, the rolled-up canvas escaped her thawing fingers and fell to the floor. Yoshiko gasped, but the other woman remained impassive.

"I'll tell the mistress that you are here." She disappeared, carrying Taizo's card on her tray.

While she waited, Yoshiko took in the high ceilings, the vivid Turkish carpets, and the ornate, gilded sconces on the walls. Such grandeur, she thought. If worse came to worst, maybe she could ask the Countess to take her on as a servant.

She was lost in a daydream of herself, warm and fed, flicking a feather duster over the frames of the paintings the lady had collected, when the Countess herself strolled into the room, a spider monkey perched on her shoulder. She struck a pose a few feet from Yoshiko, one hand cocked on her hip, the other flourishing a cigarette in a long black holder.

The woman looked Yoshiko up and down, lips curved into a faint smile. "So how is my dear little Taizo?" she asked, her voice a deep purr. "I haven't seen him around lately."

Yoshiko fought back a ripple of revulsion. "He's very well, thank you. He's working hard."

"Ah, bon I am happy to hear that." She turned back down the hallway. "Come along then. Show me what you've got." Yoshiko trailed behind.

In the parlor, the walls of which were hung with a profusion of paintings in clashing styles and colors, Yoshiko unfurled her ware. The Countess spread it across a red velvet hassock and examined it from all angles. Her gaze danced over Yoshiko's work. She seemed not to notice that parts of the painting were done by a different hand. From time to time she puffed on her cigarette, then exhaled rings of smoke. Yoshiko tried hard not to cough.

After what seemed like a month, the Countess finally looked her in the eye and said, "I like it. I'll buy it."

Yoshiko managed to get a good price for the painting. They'd be able to eat for another month or two. In the meantime, she would work on the other unfinished canvases she'd found.

––––

No one seemed to notice Yoshiko's additions, not even Taizo, who was oblivious to the disappearing paintings. Dealers continued to praise Taizo's work. Money once again flowed into their home.

And then one morning, Yoshiko woke to find her husband stiff and cold. All of his paintings had been sold or bartered. Yoshiko was alone in Paris without a *sou*.

––––

Now, standing before the last work in the gallery, Yoshiko tries hard not to think about the days spent begging at her husband's patrons' doors. She wills away the memory of her hollow stomach and the tears in the soles of her shoes.

The painting is titled "Woman, Blossoming." The date puts it at the year of Taizo's death. It shows a woman, Yoshiko, in the full flower of her beauty. But she is not like the demure Oriental odalisques of other great artists. She does not gaze wistfully off to the side while holding a fan, but straight at the viewer. She is not restricted by a cocoon-tight kimono; hers drapes loosely over her shoulders and pools on the floor.

"This is one of his best," a goateed grey-haired man says, leaning in close to examine the brushwork. "Here, he returns to the theme of his native country, but with a twist."

His companion complies. "Yes, this is so much better than that famous one of the *can-can* girls. There is such vitality here. It's as if she were about to step down from the wall."

"There's no telling what Taizo would have done had he lived longer."

The two men cast a glance at the signature in the corner of the painting and move on to the table where tea and cakes are being served.

Yoshiko remains, a Mona Lisa smile on her lips. She remembers being back in that Parisian apartment sitting before a blank canvas when she took a long look at herself in the mirror, the pink kimono loose around her shoulders when she dipped her brush in color and began to paint.

A La Carte

MARK HEATHCOTE

As a cold empty beast with a hungry heart
I seek to find you, find love and eat you.
And eat my fill, all I want a la carte
So tempt me with your eyes and come through

I want the best, so let's go 'cordon bleu.'
And howl and hoot under a blood-red moon.
I want to devour you, run-barefoot through
That meadow rue, I want to read that rune.

Find divinity, the beauty of my beast
I want her to warm me, my insides out
I want her to tease me with a love feast,
I want to be her first and last takeout.
I want to baste you in rosemary and thyme
And have you, darling, anytime-all-the time.

Here I Lie

COLLEEN MOYNE

Here I lie, taking a well-earned rest. What a thrilling and exhausting day!

Earlier this year, my companion invited me to join him on a wonderful adventure. We have been traveling through Europe, creating many new and priceless experiences and memories to share. There is so much to tell you, but let me start by describing today...

We began the morning at a sweet little café in Paris, where my companion extolled the delights of what he claimed to be the best Café Noisette in the city. He went on to explain in rapturous terms that a Noisette—French for Hazelnut—is a rich dark Espresso coffee with just a dash of cream, named so because of its hazelnut colour. Mmm...I can only lament that I am not a coffee drinker.

After savouring the pleasures of this wonderful little place, we wove our way through Paris streets brimming with character and history to the Saint-Lazare Station, where we boarded a train bound for Vernon, just over sixty kilometres to the west. The sights, sounds, and smells came alive for us both, as the train gently rocked and swayed its way through an art-scape of green countryside.

We arrived in Vernon and hailed a waiting taxi, which took us on the short journey to the famous garden of Impressionist painter, Claude Monet, in Giverny. I felt truly honoured to be sharing this experience of a lifetime with someone so sensitive and articulate as my companion. For all the photographs taken, paintings painted, and articles written about this spectacular vista, there is no one who can bring it to life better than my companion. Without so much as touching a leaf, together we tramped through the riotous flowerbeds, embraced the majestic willow trees, immersed ourselves in the tranquil lake and swam among the languid waterlilies, danced beneath the vine-draped arches, and frolicked like happy children through the sweet-smelling grasses.

At the day's end, exhausted and content, we lazily made our way back to Vernon and boarded the train that would carry us back to our Paris hotel. Cocooned in the warm railway carriage, lulled by the rhythmic whisper of the rails, we slept. And do you know the most marvellous thing about this day? It all took place within the brilliant imagination of my companion, the writer; and I, his humble servant—a simple fountain pen—conveyed it to the page. Together we work as one—a master craftsman and his instrument —to weave simple words into wonderful stories that we share with you, the reader.

How Paris Comes Back to Me

KATHRYN COCKRILL

In my head, I walk down the Rue de Castiglione,
surrounded by marble arches
and green-fronted windows,
greeted by a familiar, yet unknown, sight,
a place I hadn't been but already knew,
built in my head as a cornerstone of Paris,
Ladurée.
Rows upon rows of macarons,
one box tucked safely away in layers of tissue,
ready for the flight home,
hopefully avoiding a worser fate
of delicate almond shells in fractured pieces.

In my head, I leave the safety of Mickey Mouse
and venture through the streets,
eyeing gathering grey clouds that threaten rain
and wondering whether we're over halfway,
should we just turn back?
But we push ahead, drenched by the rain,
jeans stuck to our thighs and water dripping into
  our eyes,
Serris inching closer, 5 Place d'Ariane to be exact,
for an obsession taken 278 miles from home.

Finally, we stumble into the store, squelching in
  soggy trainers
with less-than-impressed faces,
until the fruit of our labour presents itself,
banana and lychee topped with pearls,
satisfying hungry stomachs and parched throats,
already contemplating the walk back to
  Disneylisation.
And so, Paris comes back to me
in tiny almond macarons
and rain-soaked bubble tea.

La Tour Eiffel

BHAVYA PRABHAKAR

The days have become warmer as summer
has arrived, the sun is bright as the shine
on his face, love has knocked him tight
at the stubborn dreams of his life.
He was roaming on the streets of Paris
as if he were Parisian, trying to behave
with French etiquettes, café was the only
place where he imagined her intimately
he was confused but committed to go in miles
to meet his lady love in the sunshine,
the fruits had ripened gradually
in the hope of being remembered
in the memories of shine.

His attraction towards her getting
ignited as the rocks do,
he wanted to share some space with his
lady just beneath her under the moonshine,
she is solid and hard as the mountains
but her beauty amazes millions from far
and near, his love has crossed all the boundaries
to reach this specimen of creation.

The days have become warmer as summer
has arrived, the sun is bright as the shine
on his face, love has knocked him tight
at the stubborn dreams of his life.
He was breathless and tired on the streets of Paris
waited for a long time to surrender,
in a romantic palace of stars where the moon
is hiding behind the clouds to and fro,
love was in the air as everyone was aware
of his hysteria for his lady in black.
She is all set in her attire as if the night
were shining at her best.

This summer has a charmed episode
where love has limitless desires,
there he was standing in front of his love on a
    sunny day;
La Tour Eiffel, 'O my love, I was getting paranoid
until I had seen you, touched you with my cold
    hands,
longed for you under the moonshine.'

Lilia in the Metro or A Visit to Versailles

SUZANNE KAMATA

I know that Sunday isn't the best day for a visit to one of France's premier tourist attractions. The website suggests that it will be mobbed, and I'm worried about the weather. If it's sunny, or at least not raining, we will go.

The question is how to get there?

My twelve-year-old daughter, Lilia, who I have brought along on this trip, uses a wheelchair.

Originally, I planned on going by taxi or hiring a guide for door-to-door service. But I don't really want a guided tour. Without Japanese Sign Language, or at least Japanese, Lilia wouldn't be able to understand anyway. And the metro would be way cheaper than taking a taxi.

By day three, I'm feeling more confident about our ability to get around. I noticed an elevator at the Bir Hakim train station, and I discovered that many of the major metro stations are wheelchair accessible. Line 14 is fully accessible, in accordance with new French laws. And, if nothing else, the metro will be an essential Parisian experience.

After a leisurely breakfast of *pain au chocolat*, sliced pears, and ham, I push the wheelchair down the street toward the Eiffel Tower and the Bir Hakim train station. I'd assumed that metro maps for wheelchair users would be available throughout Paris, but that's not the case. After standing in front of the ticket vending machine for a few minutes, trying to figure out how to buy a ticket to Versailles with my credit card, I give up and go to the window.

I have heard that the French are rude to tourists, but the guy in the ticket window has infinite patience. Even though there is a line growing behind me, he remains calm when I can't remember my PIN number. He comes out from behind the booth and helps me buy tickets from the vending machine, then he draws our route on a map. We'll have to change trains a couple of times in order to get onto Line 14. When I can't figure out how to get through the gate to the elevator, even though the directions are written clearly on a sign (Silly me! I didn't read the sign!), he helps us through the gate, all the while maintaining perfect composure.

I realize that maybe I am becoming a little bit too dependent upon the kindness of strangers. There was a time when I would have been able to figure everything out all by myself. Special treatment because of Lilia's wheelchair is making me soft. Or maybe it's just because I've spent so many years living in Japan where people are always quick to help, where as soon as I open a map, a stranger will offer to show me the way. Then again, bringing my daughter to France was something of an accomplishment, wasn't it? And accepting assistance when I need it isn't such a bad thing.

Lilia has been to cities with underground railways before—Tokyo, Osaka, Washington D.C.—but this will be her first ever ride on a subway. I maneuver her wheelchair onto the metro car. Knees move aside to make room. Lilia puts on her brakes, and the train surges toward the next station. Opposite us, an older woman sits, eyes downcast. A young mother wrangles her small child. A group of brightly dressed tourists—Americans?—cling to the poles.

We are all absorbed with our own thoughts, thinking ahead, perhaps, to a day at work, a playdate, a morning of sightseeing. Just then, a shaggy-haired guy, with a guitar slung over his shoulder, steps into the car. Great. There goes my peace and quiet. And he'll probably come around with a cup, asking for money.

Lilia eyes him with curiosity. This is something totally new to her. Although I've seen street performers in Tokyo, and even in front of the Tokushima train station, there are signs in the subway system prohibiting buskers. He begins to strum. Lilia starts to nod and clap along with him. Realizing that he has an audience, he sings directly to her, a serenade to my thirteen-year-old daughter. I fight the urge to still her hands and divert her attention.

The older woman across from us smiles at her, and so does the harried young mother. I give in to the moment, until a grin spreads across my face, as well.

At the next stop, the man crosses the car and says something to Lilia before getting off. He doesn't know that she can't hear him. We don't give him any money; he doesn't ask for any. "Au revoir," Lilia says, waving and waving until he is out of sight.

So now we have to find the correct exit and our next metro. We go to the end of the platform to find stairs. We go to the other end... more stairs. Now I'm confused. Hadn't the guy shown us an accessible route? Does "accessible" mean something different to the French? If we go up the wrong steps, we'll have to come back down. And what if I made a mistake, and we got off at the wrong stop entirely? There's no one around to ask. I have a horrible vision of being stuck in the metro for hours—a version of hell.

I finally make a decision. We'll try the shorter of the two staircases.

"Can you climb up those steps?" I ask Lilia. There are only about five, and there's a railing that she can hang on to.

She nods. Well, she managed the staircase at the Hotel Biron. This will be cake. She gets out of her wheelchair and grabs onto the railing. I carry the wheelchair up to the top and set it down at an angle so she'll be able to sit down. At the top, we find the stairs to the next platform. It's a busier stop, and lots of commuters are bustling past us. There are more stairs than before, but going down is always easier than going up.

I park the wheelchair at the top of the stairs. "Ready?" I ask.

Lilia nods gamely.

But just before she's about to get up again, a pair of young men rush over and volunteer to help. It all happens so fast. They heft Lilia and her wheelchair like an ancient empress's palanquin and deposit her safely at the bottom of the steps.

"Merci!" I call after them. "Merci beaucoup!"

In the train station, I find a woman worker and ask for help. She tells me that the elevator to the platform we need isn't working. The train will have to be diverted to another track, but she and another worker will help us board.

"She'll have to step down at Versailles," the woman warns.

"She can do that," I say. "I'll help her."

When it's time to board, the workers set up a gangway going from the platform to the train. Steps lead up or down to the seats, so we'll have to wait near the door. There's no place for me to sit. Oh, well. It might be uncomfortable for a little while, but it's cheaper than taking a taxi or a private tour. Plus, it's an adventure.

At the stop for Versailles, another kind Frenchman helps us off the train and shows us to the slightly difficult-to-find ramp that leads out of the station. Then, after what seems like hours underground and enclosed, we stepped into the chilly, spring day.

To find our way to the palace, all we have to do is follow the hordes. People from all over the world—China, Japan, America, other European countries speaking languages I can't identify—are surging toward Versailles. If this is the off-season, I hate to imagine how crowded it would be during a Sunday in high season.

We pass a street performer—a guy dressed like an Egyptian mummy. His skin is golden, his eyes dramatically outlined. And he is as stoic as those British guys in bear hats outside Buckingham Palace. A bucket for coins is positioned in front of him.

When we get to the gates of Versailles, a guard directs us to the entrance for the disabled. We bump over the cobblestones, past long lines of tourists waiting to get in. And then finally, we are inside.

"*Tabetai*," Lilia signs. *I'm hungry.*

It's already noon, but the only food I can find are the macarons at the Laduree shop near the entrance. *"Let them eat cake!"* Tempting, but we need something more substantial. In order to get to the restaurants, we'll have to go through the palace first.

"Can you wait just a little while?" I ask her.

She nods.

Because we have recently watched Sophia Coppola's *Marie Antoinette*, in which Kirsten Dunst-as-the-queen runs down deserted corridors, I find the large number of visitors disconcerting. I'd somehow imagined Lilia and me alone in the Hall of 578 Mirrors, reflected ad infinitum, or wandering the gardens quietly instead of trying to stay out of other people's snapshots. The Hall of Mirrors, created in 1686, once represented the economic and cultural power of France and the society of the royal court where seeing and being seen, preferably in one's most gorgeous gown, were so important. On this day, however, the mirrors multiply hordes of tourists. In order to see anything at all, we'll have to fight our way to the front.

Lilia doesn't seem bothered by the crush of humanity or the disconnect between fantasy and reality. She doesn't seem to overly mind her wheelchair-level view of hundreds of bottoms from around the world. *Au contraire.* She looks up, up, up and notices the painted ceilings, which are indeed splendid. Glittery chandeliers drip down, and images of well-fed angels floating on billowy clouds are framed in gilt, along with full-color scenes celebrating the first years of the reign of Louis XIV.

Luckily, there are attentive docents, mostly young men, on hand down below. Whenever one of them sees Lilia's wheelchair, he creates a path to the main attraction. Lilia gets a good look at Marie Antoinette's bed with its floral tapestry cover, which she recognizes from the movie, and the table where the King and Queen publicly dined.

By the time we've seen the requisite sites and posed for the obligatory photo in the Hall of Mirrors, we are faint with hunger. We head for Angelina's for croque monsieur sandwiches and its trademark African hot chocolate. (A little history: Angelina's was once called Rumpelmayers. It was once a favorite hang-out of Audrey Hepburn and Coco Chanel.)

The hot chocolate, so rich and thick that you could almost eat it with a fork, comes with a generous side dish of whipped cream. Although one website warned that the wait staff at Angelina's Tea Room doesn't speak much English, our waiter is fluent. I even hear him speaking Japanese to the two guys at the next table.

After lunch, we take a little train past grazing sheep in green pastures and visitors on bicycles to le Grand Trianon. Napoleon Bonaparte once made this his residence, as did Charles de Gaulle.

The crowd is thinner here so we're able to wander more freely. Lilia sets herself up in front of the ornate gate and begins sketching.

Once inside, we're permitted to go beyond the velvet ropes of one room, while other tourists snap photos from behind the barrier. I wonder how many strangers' photo albums we will appear in.

We still haven't gotten to Le Petit Trianon, Marie Antoinette's playhouse, but it's getting late and I'm tired. We still have to take the train and subway back to Paris, and I want to save a little bit of energy.

"Is it okay if we go back to the hotel?" I ask Lilia.

She nods, but I can tell she's a little disappointed.

"We'll come again," I tell her. "We'll see Marie Antoinette's house next time." Having made it this far, another visit no longer seems outside the realm of possibility.

We get back on the little train and return to the palace where we take a few final photos of the gushing fountains and the sprawling lawn. And then I push Lilia back down the hill, over the bumpy cobblestones, and through the gauntlet of Africans selling Eiffel Tower keychains. The street performer dressed as an Egyptian mummy is still there, outside the gates. As far as I can tell, he's been there all day, in the exact same position. Impressive.

"Here." I hand Lilia a euro. "Put this in the bucket."

She rolls over to the performer and drops the coin in with the others, then poses for a photo. The "mummy" doesn't move.

I wonder how long he will stay here. Maybe he's been coming every day for years. Maybe someday I'll finally find a full-time job in Japan and we'll have enough money to come back to this place, to check out the rest of Versailles, and this street performer will still be here.

Loves a Ballet Dance

MARK HEATHCOTE

Loves a ballet dance
it's a slippery romance
its thunder and lightning
it's a feeling that leads to tribalism
it's Beauty & the Beast
west meets east.

Loves a ballet dance
it's a hard-fought stance
it's Margot Fonteyn,
meeting with elephantine
feet that can't keep a rhythm,
without a head-on collision.

Loves a ballet dance
and like 'Gay Paree' France
there are moments of beauty
that is if-you're-not-too, choosy
shall immortalize your appreciation
you're too short a life duration.

Loves a ballet dance
a reckless circumstance
sometimes with guile, we glide
at other times we tap-dance
in our hobnail boots,
we stick together even if it persecutes.

Mons Martyrum

KATRENIA BUSCH

Departed of the body—
The mind began to soar—
From the flesh of the psyche
It was the spirit it wore—

Where the spirit obeyed
The flesh and mind
When a saint had prayed
Leaving the world behind

Mother of Chemistry

REX MCGREGOR

SYNOPSIS:
Paris, 1794. The Reign of Terror is at its height. Antoine Lavoisier, "The Father of Chemistry," is facing the guillotine. Marie-Anne, his wife and laboratory partner, desperately tries to save his life.

CHARACTERS:
ANTOINE LAVOISIER, scientist, 50
MARIE-ANNE LAVOISIER, scientist, 36
LOUIS SAINT-JUST, politician, 26
NANOU (MARIE-ANNE LENORMAND), fortune teller, 21

SETTING: A cell in the Conciergerie Prison, Paris
TIME: May 8, 1794

Antoine contemplates a laurel wreath. He places it on his head and adopts a mock haughty pose. He smiles, takes off the wreath and calmly accepts his fate.

(Marie-Anne enters, flourishing a document.)

MARIE-ANNE: A testimonial. From Lamarck!

ANTOINE: He disputes my work.

MARIE-ANNE: He respects your integrity.

ANTOINE: Goodness.

MARIE-ANNE: Even your rivals support you.

ANTOINE: It's too late.

MARIE-ANNE: The court can't ignore this.

ANTOINE: Marie-Anne, they've pronounced the verdict. The guillotine.

MARIE-ANNE: No!

ANTOINE: The others, too.

MARIE-ANNE: My father?

ANTOINE: You have double cause to weep.

MARIE-ANNE: I'll grieve for him once I've rescued you.

ANTOINE: My love! You can't charm the guard to let me out.

MARIE-ANNE: I've written to the whole Committee. Surely there's one educated man amongst them.

ANTOINE: An unverified hypothesis.

MARIE-ANNE: How can you joke?

ANTOINE: I go to the block within the hour.

MARIE-ANNE: That's outrageous! They must grant time for an appeal.

ANTOINE: They need these cells for more victims.

MARIE-ANNE: Savages! I supported the Revolution. Now it's drowning in blood.

ANTOINE: Hold on to your ideals. I can face death, knowing you'll be safe.

MARIE-ANNE: What good is safety to a childless widow?

ANTOINE: Remarry. You may yet be blessed.

MARIE-ANNE: I can never become pregnant.

ANTOINE: Wait and see.

MARIE-ANNE: Antoine... I tried for years. With another man.

ANTOINE: Pierre.

MARIE-ANNE: You knew?

ANTOINE: He used to envy me. One day, he stopped.

MARIE-ANNE: Forgive me. I was desperate for a baby.

(*Antoine embraces Marie-Anne tenderly.*)

ANTOINE: We've created something together. Something that will live on after us. Our work.

MARIE-ANNE: *Our* work?

ANTOINE: I couldn't have made my... *We* couldn't have made *our* discoveries without you.

MARIE-ANNE: It's been the joy of my life to document your experiments.

ANTOINE: You did more than sketch. You translated Priestley. Pointing out his errors.

MARIE-ANNE: That fool. Still believes in phlogiston.

ANTOINE: You'll have a tough job converting him.

MARIE-ANNE: What?

ANTOINE: You must continue our work, Marie-Anne. Take it to the world.

MARIE-ANNE: You know that's not possible. It's illegal for a woman to practice chemistry.

ANTOINE: Never stopped you before.

MARIE-ANNE: I was your laboratory assistant.

ANTOINE: Partner.

MARIE-ANNE: Besides, they've confiscated all our equipment.

ANTOINE: Reclaim it.

MARIE-ANNE: I don't need test tubes, Antoine. I need *you*!

ANTOINE: My students crowned me with this. It's yours now.

(*Antoine moves to crown Marie-Anne. She resists.*)

MARIE-ANNE: No.

ANTOINE: Spread our legacy.

MARIE-ANNE: I can't.

ANTOINE: You must.

MARIE-ANNE: I can only mourn.

(*Marie-Anne throws the wreath on the floor. Louis and Nanou enter, arm in arm.*)

LOUIS: Citizen Lavoisier! An honor to meet you at last.

(*Louis extends his hand. Confused; Antoine grants a handshake.*)

ANTOINE: Er...

LOUIS: Louis Saint-Just.

MARIE-ANNE: From the Committee?

LOUIS: At your service. Your letter was most eloquent.

MARIE-ANNE: I didn't expect someone so...

LOUIS: Young?

MARIE-ANNE: Polite.

LOUIS: Ha! I'm only twenty-six and I've already been president of the National Convention.

NANOU: Don't brag, Louis.

LOUIS: I stand rebuked. No politician can match the eminence of Citizen Lavoisier.

NANOU: Who's he again?

LOUIS: The Father of Chemistry! He discovered—what-do-you-call-it?—the stuff you breathe.

NANOU: Air?

ANTOINE: Oxygen.

NANOU: Never heard of it.

LOUIS: Hide your ignorance, Nanou! It reflects on me.

ANTOINE: Someday, everyone in the world will be enlightened.

NANOU: Pouah! That's not how you predict the future. Gotta be specific.

LOUIS: Citizens. I present Mam'zelle Lenormand.

MARIE-ANNE: The fortune teller?

NANOU: She's heard of me, Louis. And I'm only twenty-one.

MARIE-ANNE: Your tarot readings are the talk of the town. Do you have your cards with you?

NANOU: Always. Would you like a session?

MARIE-ANNE: I'd like to examine the deck, if I may.

NANOU: Feel free.

(*Nanou hands a deck of tarot cards to Marie-Anne.*)

MARIE-ANNE: No doubt you use sleight of hand. Each card marked on the back?

NANOU: I can do readings blindfold.

MARIE-ANNE: So it's by touch. Different textures?

NANOU: I don't need cards at all.

LOUIS: My theory is she senses—what-do-you-call-'em?—spiritual emanations.

MARIE-ANNE: Hogwash!

LOUIS: Her prophecies are extremely accurate. How do you account for that?

MARIE-ANNE: She reads people—don't you, my dear?

NANOU: Can't give away trade secrets.

MARIE-ANNE: Admit it. You're a cheap swindler.

LOUIS: Now hold on!

MARIE-ANNE: You gullible fool. Test her. Under controlled conditions.

LOUIS: If she's a fraud, I'll lock her up myself.

NANOU: You're such a prig, Louis. I've gone right off you.

(*Nanou grabs her cards. A distant bell tolls.*)

LOUIS: We'll settle this later. Your time has come, Citizen. If you'll be so kind...

(*Louis takes a cord from his pocket. Antoine presents his wrists.*)

MARIE-ANNE: What are you doing?

LOUIS: Behind your back, please. Much more dignified.

(*Antoine puts his hands behind his back. Louis ties them.*)

MARIE-ANNE: I... I thought you were here to set him free.

LOUIS: No. I came to shake the hand of a great man. And personally escort him to the scaffold.

MARIE-ANNE: Surely you appreciate how important he is to France!

LOUIS: To the entire world! This is a lamentable day for science.

MARIE-ANNE: Then you'll intervene?

LOUIS: We're not killing Lavoisier the chemist. We're executing Lavoisier the corrupt tax collector.

ANTOINE: I acted within the law.

LOUIS: The wall around Paris was your idea, was it not?

ANTOINE: To control the flow of goods.

LOUIS: To fleece honest merchants and line your pockets!

MARIE-ANNE: Malicious lies!

LOUIS: Enough! — Citizen, you must accept the inevitable.

ANTOINE: I do. — Marie-Anne. Let us say farewell.

MARIE-ANNE: No! No!

(Marie-Anne clings to Antoine in distress.)

ANTOINE: I abandon all hope of glory. All vain ambition.

LOUIS: Spoken like a stoic. I admire you.

ANTOINE: No one else will. My reputation will vanish. As insubstantial as... phlogiston.

NANOU: Flodge-what?

LOUIS: Phlogiston. The stuff that makes things burn— *(To Antoine)* I know my chemistry.

ANTOINE: I leave the world to men such as you. Who spurn superstition.

LOUIS: There speaks a scientist! Calm and rational.

MARIE-ANNE: I'm only a woman. Prone to sentiment. Soldiers took away my husband's things. Weird-shaped flasks and whatnot.

LOUIS: Oh dear.

MARIE-ANNE: If I could have them back, it would be some consolation.

LOUIS: Leave it to me. I'm actually in favor of women owning property. Call me a radical.

(Nanou picks up the wreath and offers it to Antoine.)

NANOU: Is this yours?

ANTOINE: It was.

LOUIS: I'm afraid the executioner doesn't permit any head covering.

NANOU: I'll have it. The classical look's in fashion.

MARIE-ANNE: Give it here!

(*Marie-Anne snatches the wreath and puts it on.*)

LOUIS: Um. Is such adornment appropriate? For an imminent widow?

MARIE-ANNE: Apollo wore the first laurel wreath in mourning for his love.

ANTOINE: I always thought it was a symbol of triumph.

MARIE-ANNE: Later on.

LOUIS: Scholarly debate. How stoic!

MARIE-ANNE: May we have one last minute, alone?

LOUIS: Of course. Nanou, out!

(*Nanou huffs and exits. Louis bows and exits. Marie-Anne and Antoine share an emotional moment.*)

ANTOINE: Brava.

MARIE-ANNE: I shall be a good mother. Of chemistry.

End of play.

Night at the Theater

SUZANNE KAMATA

We've come for the pig mask
poker, the rabbit costumes,
the Japanese mime on stage.
At the entrance we are directed to
an elevator that will lift us to
accessible seating. My daughter boards
in her wheelchair, I step in after.
An usher reaches inside, pushes
a button, says "Get off when the elevator
stops," in French. We rise, doors whoosh
open to an empty, dark hall, a rock
garden, a locked passageway.
We wait but no one comes. My daughter
forms questions with her fingers. The hands
on my watch indicate ten minutes
past the hour. The performance is now
underway.

Notre Dame

MICHAEL CAMARILLO

our lady of paris
endures the flames
on a week of spiritual pain
history in its suffering
its spire to God taken
by the fire as its people
surround its glowing frame
singing as one glory to her
the benediction of faith
in her resurrection
to hold her city
in her arms once more

Parisian Streets and the French Connection

BHAVYA PRABHAKAR

The connection was innocent with Parisian streets; I fumbled many times to catch hold of my breath in the unknown territory. I felt aloof, yet, enjoying the fragrance of trees and mud, the only thing talking was the natural bodies. The amazement in the eyes kept me astonished at the gloomy shades of the sky, the clouds were familiar to me. I tasted the same ease being in contact with them. Parisian streets were crowded, hugely populated with different nationalities. I was afraid of some of the faces in the metro; the continuous gazing was making the ambience uncomfortable. The French were as beautiful as the red roses, the French language is my dearest of all which taught me the meaning of reading and writing. French literature has given me the horizon to comprehend the literary theories and the essence of writing all together.

The connection was innocent with Parisian streets; I fumbled many times to catch hold of my breath in the unknown territory. I felt aloof, yet enjoying the falling leaves and the sudden rains; peeping through the window to see the cats and the people was like an extraordinary affair; in the meantime, people were running at full speed to be updated to the muscles in the company of some good music. I was afraid of black color, yet I could make good bond with the blacks and the blondes. The residence was full of multicultural attires; the sharing kitchen was my only point of interaction with some unknown faces of that time. I was frightened and amazed to meet some with the Almighty connection and beliefs; the love for Parisian culture is like loving the smell of wine, giving an oozing effect without drinking its capacity.

The connection was innocent with Parisian streets; I fumbled many times to catch hold of my breath in the unknown territory. I felt aloof, yet exploring the beauties together: La Tour Eiffel and Notre Dame de Paris, the sky was at its best in the shadows of clouds. Champs- Élysées, attracting the throng, I was lost in the paradise of kingdom where life is as easy as a roller coaster. Bonjour is the word that kept reminding me of the existence of self in a foreign land. French language has its own uniqueness; eyes were the ocean of my observation which has given me wings to fly.

The connection was innocent with Parisian streets; I fumbled many times to catch hold of my breath in the unknown territory. I felt aloof, yet exploring the world in the company of some strange soul kept me in love in the conditions unknown. The feeling is mutual today; the realism triggers the society with the future plans. Paris was a dream of many that came true in the excitement of yesterday; I found myself with the destiny of mine, where goals and ambitions are coinciding with the straight forwardness of some. The connection was and is growing with Parisian streets and its people, where things may be blurred but not the memories of thine: Parisian streets.

This poem was first published at Spillwords.com, on 5th May 2021.

Foiled

LINDA DICKMAN

For all those affected by the Nov.13, 2015 attack in Paris

Before you Lord, the wicked
Fall and none shall dwell
Within your hall. The proud shall
Never gain a place, nor evil like to see your face.
(As Morning Dawns – Fred R. Anderson)

His breath, like explosions
 scattered flocks,
café's customers and *accouterments*
spill out in every direction along
la voie des ténèbres.

Attackers *become* the dark eagles of death,
tearing flesh by pushing buttons
sirens the new heavy metal,
concert goers escape -
everywhere a foot fall,
a foot fell.

Injured fruit wrapped in gold foil,
pour le voyage à l'hôpital
a gleaming trail to healing.

Destruction brought us together,
death begat prayer,
deliberate forgiveness
though incomplete.

Le visage de Satan showing briefly.
Each glance brought death.
Each stare born from intolerance.
Each squint sealing the real perpetrator.

Spitting loss, spontaneous
broken hallelujahs all around
Empty shoes glittering in the night,
like stars guiding the dancers home.

The holy one says,
fast on fear, feast on faith.
Mercy, grace for their souls,
seventy times seven for the sinner.

Vous! Malin the whole time your fly was open.

The Days of Lafayette

BHAVYA PRABHAKAR

The days of *Lafayette[1]*, *TV5[2]*, *promenade[3]*, *voyage, visite[4]*, *pronunciation,* in the petit studio of my residence, it was strange and absurd, gazing from the window, the clouds were cozy and dense, the monuments and the attractions were kind of amazing discoveries, the nude statues, *le café[5]*, *la baguette[6]*, *le fromage[7]*. The smell of the European land was surreal as if I had known this land for ages.

The days *of Lafayette, TV5, promenade, voyage, visite, pronunciation,* and of course the Francophone Literature; my classes were full of diversities with different origins, my black friend wanted to greet me like a Frenchman. The awkwardness gathered inside me for a while under the pressure of Indian culture which was so dominant.

The days of *cigarette, Paris, métro, gare[8], tram, Carrefour[9]* took me into the caves of the sudden collapse of the images which I portrayed in the TGV[10], an amazing rapid train in which I could ever sit with observant surroundings; people thronged to travel, reading books and listening to music; I felt different and my skin color defined me in the crowd.

The days of *bla bla car, Montpellier[11], Paris, Sète[12], Tours[13]*; the voyage defined me all except that hidden foul image with which I lived there, with the hope to settle there one day, I was contented of behaving like a dominant one, despite knowing that reliance on people or things can turn into disaster; the failure of broken wings kept reminding me that I took the place with me except that image.

The days of *Lafayette, TV5, promenade, voyage, visite, Montpellier, Paris* gave me a sense of traveling and understanding away from the homeland; people may change according to the time but places remain unaltered in the lane of memories.

---

[1] Lafayette—a French surname. There are cities, places, buildings, businesses, and hotels with this name. In this poem, the reference is to Galeries Lafayette, a department store chain that is shown as a great memory of France.

[2] TV5—French TV channel

[3] Promenade—walk in French

[4] Visite—visit in French

[5] Le café – cafe or coffee

[6] La baguette—French bread

[7] Le fromage—cheese in French

[8] Gare—station (train)

[9] Carrefour—name of a supermarket

[10] TGV—rapid train, name of the train

[11] Montpellier—French city

[12] Sète—French city

[13] Tours—French city

Paris: A Student Experience in Travel

KIM POULOS LIEBERZ

We were in our early 20s and traveling with our Eurail passes. A group of art school students from FIT in New York City studying in Florence and out to see the world. We went everywhere we could afford to; we stayed in youth hostels and cheap hotels and had no idea what we were doing or where we were going, but adventure was calling. Wanderlust. We had paper maps, used cash that we exchanged at the train stations, and, of course, had no cell phones. How primitive.

It was the winter of 1987; the year and our semester abroad were ending, and we had yet to go to Paris. How could we miss it? A group of us planned our trip, jumped on a train with our backpacks and student ids, and headed to France.

I was worried that we did not speak the language, though having been in Italy for the past three months, I had a good handle on my Italian, but French, though a romance language, was foreign to me, primarily because of the accent. I could count, say bon jour, bon soir and je m'appelle Kim, all thanks to my fourth-grade French program, but that was basically it, and I wanted to be able to navigate the city and its sites. My French accent, however, was not very good at all. And all you heard was that the French don't like Americans. "The people in Paris will be rude to you." We'd all heard it before, even in 1987, and everyone felt they should warn us about it.

But I didn't worry as I have always felt when traveling and in life, if you go to a place and are unfriendly, you will find unfriendly people. And if you go with a friendly attitude, you will find the nicest, friendliest people.

So off to France we went, four of us jammed into a cubby-like seating on the overnight train. There was a couple with us. They were a little older than us, brother and sister traveling back home to Paris. We spent the entire train ride speaking, and they tried to teach us as much French as possible. I took notes and practiced with them. I am sure I sounded terrible, but they were very encouraging. We talked about life and art and where we were from. They helped us plan how to get to our hostel, what we should see during our weekend, and other helpful travel tips. But I remember the most how they were so patient and determined to teach me French. I got down a few more phrases and became slightly more confident. We exchanged addresses and home phone numbers and went on our way.

These French siblings were kind and encouraging. I felt they truly appreciated my attempt to learn their language. We were humans interested in each other, sharing our differences and learning about our cultures.

We arrived later in the day, tired from the trip but excited to be in Paris. The first thing I remember that has stayed with me all these years is the light. The sky is just different there. I can't explain it. The hue of the sky was soft and pastel. How the light illuminated buildings and the landscape was just spectacular. It was like being in a painting. We had an inspiring time walking along the Champs des Lyons. In the evening, at a café, we met a group of young French guys our age. We had fun flirting and trying to communicate as best we could. As it got later and later, we had to get back to our hostel, but we were quite far away. The guys offered to give us a ride. We were New York girls, so we had to play it safe. Of course, we were nervous, so we split them up and kept a few of them back to stay with us while the others went to the hostel. Then, the rest of us went on the second ride. They were just nice guys willing to help us out. No strings, just kindness. Looking back, and of course, after the way the world has changed and the movies I have seen, maybe it was crazy, but maybe it was just people helping people.

The next day, we did all the typical tourist things. We ate crepes on the street, my favorite, Nutella. We went to the Louvre and saw the Mona Lisa amongst so many other masterpieces that we had been studying as art school students. To see them in person was just fantastic. We went to the Eiffel Tower where, towards the top, we met a guy from Brooklyn; New York is everywhere.

Our excursion to Paris was only a few days, but it was a fun, educational, and memorable experience that has stayed with me all these years. Reminiscing on it still renews my faith in humanity. We are all just trying to have a good life: travel, enjoy some experiences, see new things, and learn about the world. Ninety-nine percent of the people you meet are interested in you and willing to welcome and help you. And as I had found, especially in France.

For a few years afterward, the brother and sister from the train and I sent each other holiday cards. I am so glad I said Bon Jour that day on the Eurail train, even if said it poorly.

If It Waddles and Quacks, Is It a Duck?

DONNA KEEL ARMER

Paris, in my opinion, is the *duckdom* of the world. Most people go to Paris to see the Eiffel Tower, the Arc de Triomphe, the Louvre, Notre Dame, and numerous other tourist attractions. I went to Paris to eat duck.

Prior to meeting my husband, I had never eaten duck. I also had never been to Paris, two events he made it his mission to correct. The fact that I was not a wine drinker appeared on his list too, but he tackled that well before we were married. The duck came next and finally Paris.

French pinot noir paired with duck was my first lesson. The meal was simple yet complex. Simple because there were only a few ingredients, complex because it took time to prepare the duck while striving to create the perfect flavor profile. Did I mention that my husband is a terrific cook?

He taught me that pinot noir and duck have flavors of moderate intensity. The acid in the pinot noir balances the fattiness of the duck. It is also standard protocol to cook duck (according to my chef-to-be husband) with some type of fruit, either a fruit sauce or fruit accompaniment to match the fruity notes of the pinot.

243

The duck salad Ray whipped up for me was only one of the many reasons that I married him. Crisp greens, thin slices of medium rare duck, Gorgonzola, toasted walnuts, pears, and a raspberry vinaigrette, served, of course, with pinot noir. As I raved about the meal, he humbly said, "Yes, it's good but wait until you have duck in Paris."

At the end of the meal, I was looking for the marriage contract, wondering why this man was available. He wasn't for long.

In the early years of our marriage, we were avid cooks of all things French. We subscribed to every gourmet magazine. It was in one of the gourmet magazines that we discovered Brasserie du Théâtre Montanseir in Versailles, France. There was a big spread featuring duck confit. Thoughts of a trip to Paris began to percolate.

The excitement of planning and the romantic notion of Paris kept me in a state of ecstasy. I floated through workdays. On the weekends I organized what we would see and do in the few days we'd be in Paris as we had also planned to rent a car and visit the Champagne region.

About ten days before our departure, my husband broke his ankle on a morning jog when a car nearly side-swiped him. Without much sympathy, I looked him in the eye and said, "I'm going to Paris with or without you. You decide."

He convinced the orthopedic doctor to discard the hard cast for a soft one. This man was not going to miss feeding me the best duck ever. He was a trooper and did not allow his shrouded leg to limit his mobility. The one good thing about his accident was he couldn't drive so we changed our plans to spend all our time in Paris.

We stayed in a quaint, boutique hotel in the first arrondissement. We toured the Louvre, visited the Arc de Triomphe and Notre Dame, took a night cruise on the Seine, and raised champagne glasses in the rain as the twinkling lights of the Eiffel Tower illuminated the foggy sky. And, we ate duck.

After numerous duck feasts, we were still looking for that best duck dish. On our last day in Paris, we hopped (me) and limped (Ray) onto a train headed to the Palace of Versailles. Both the palace and the duck confit at Brasserie de Théâtre Montansier met our stringent expectations.

The duck confit was juicy, tender, and creamy with a satisfyingly crispy skin. Tiny potatoes roasted in duck fat nestled along side, and the proverbial haricots verts (French green beans) arrived on a separate platter splashing buttery, garlicky goodness.

The meal was only slightly spoiled by a standard black French poodle who shared the banquette next to me. After I was seated, I felt movement on the bench and turned to smile at whomever was seated beside me. I was startled by a wet snout inches from my face. He sniffed the air around me, pulled back, and turned away. Clearly I was not worthy of a tête-à-tête with this noble creature.

But the meal was a huge success. On our last night, we ventured out for a last hand-in-hand stroll along the Seine and one last breath-taking view of the lighting of the Eiffel Tower sans rain. And we murmured sweet nothings about our duck feast.

Paris, in my opinion, is not a one-time adventure. The City of Lights stayed with me, residing in some obscure file stored away in my long-term memory. It would be eighteen years before we returned. We were certainly older and had far more travel experience in our luggage than we had when we'd embarked on our first blissful duck trip so many years earlier.

The huge difference in this next trip was that we had retired. We would be staying in France over six weeks: two weeks in Paris, one week self-piloting a boat down the Canal du Midi, and three weeks in Provence and then we would wrap up the trip with a couple more nights in Paris. Our plan was to eat duck.

So much had happened to the world in those ensuing years with the major horrific event being 9/11. Flying was no longer an event we looked forward to yet this two-leg flight was seamless. Everything was on time including the luggage and the van to take us to our apartment in the 2nd arrondissement. The only shock was we left South Carolina with temperatures in the 90s and landed in Paris where they had plummeted into the 30s with gale force winds. As soon as our luggage arrived, we plundered it for warmer clothing although lightweight rain jackets were all we'd packed. After all it was May in Paris. Wasn't it supposed to be warm?

Using an American VIP agency, I had booked our apartment in the second arrondissement near rue Montorgueil, one of the best market streets in Paris with the oldest pâtisserie (Stohrer). I chose this agency for one reason only. They had a policy of mailing the keys of the apartment you rented along with the outside code to enter the building. Instead of waiting until late afternoon to check-in, this agency gave us permission to enter the apartment as soon as we arrived in Paris. How clever was that to arrive at 6:30 a.m. and immediately be able to settle into our apartment?

I continued to ask myself that question as I sat on an icy cold marble floor in the foyer instead of being safely ensconced in our warm abode. Upon arrival, we keyed in the code we had been given, and the outside door opened into a small foyer. A glass door stood between the foyer and our apartment. It was locked and none of the keys we had been sent would open it.

Yes, of course, we were prepared. We rang the agent in Paris once we determined that the cell phone reception didn't work in the foyer. My foot kept the outside door propped open while Ray made the call that immediately rolled to a message service. After all, it's way too early in the morning for a French person to be up.

We waited—me on the cold floor, Ray pacing the 6'x6' foyer. He had to go to the bathroom, and he sorely needed coffee. Our first conference (one of many) included me staying behind with the luggage to wait on the agent who after two hours still hadn't shown up. Ray took care of business, placed another call to the agent and returned with a slightly lukewarm cup of coffee.

While he was gone, I added more layers to my skimpy sleeveless shirt and sat on a pair of jeans to help ease the cold that penetrated every bone in my achy body. The building across the street stirred into life. Large doors opened revealing a sidewalk bar and a tiny cafe. This time Ray stayed with the luggage and I ventured across.

The owner spoke a little English, enough so that I was able to persuade him to place another call to the agent.

"I'm on my way," came the snappish response.

Just as I returned to the foyer, a man in a rush pushed through the glass door. I grabbed it and voila, we were inside the building. I held the glass door open while Ray hauled all our luggage through. Besides the great opportunity to have the key to our apartment was the fact that this building had an elevator. We were all smiles as we passed the well-worn stone steps leading up in a narrow circular pattern. The instructions the agency provided said to take the elevator to the 3rd floor (4th by American standards), then turn left and the apartment was at the end of the corridor.

I took two years of French at university which was so many years ago that my vocabulary only consisted of the following phrases: *merci* (thank you), *s'il vous plaît* (please), *pardon moi* (excuse me), *je m'excuse* (I'm sorry), and the ultimate phrase *où se trouvent les toilette* (where is the bathroom). This lack of all but the most basic vocabulary limited my ability to read the large sign on the elevator that stated *l'ascenseur est en panne*. But it didn't take a rocket scientist to figure out the elevator was broken.

Ray and I had a second conference. I was designated to take the keys, climb the many steps, locate our apartment and return to assist Ray with the luggage. After flying for hours, a six hour time difference, a drastic change in the weather, and sitting on an icy cold marble floor for two hours, my body whined as I climbed the ancient staircase.

There didn't seem to be any indication of what floor I'd reached and so far none of the apartments had numbers, names or any identifiable markings so that I'd know I was at the correct place. I rang doorbells. No one answered. Each time I tried every key on the keyring but none fit. I tried another floor. This time when I rang the doorbell, a tousled haired man still in pajamas opened the door and yelled something impolite in French. I mumbled *je m'excuse* and fled down the steps.

We had a third conference and agreed that it made far more sense to drag our luggage across the street and wait in the friendly little bar which overlooked our apartment entry. A glass of wine to warm our frozen bodies seemed a heavenly option although it was only 10:30 in the morning. We gathered our luggage and proceeded.

Before we could drag all our luggage back into the foyer and out the front door, the street cleaners arrived and began to hose down the street. We stood on the curb debating. We each had a large piece of luggage, a small carry-on, and miscellaneous stuff. We watched the ankle-deep water flow swiftly past our already cold and tired feet.

Our smiles were feeble as we plunged our feet into the icy flow and sloughed across the small river. Eating duck did not come to mind as we gingerly waddled across to the other side while the street cleaners looked on with amusement. Drinking wine did come to mind, and we did—drink wine. It was another hour before the agent showed up. After two glasses of wine, we were certainly in a better mood and perhaps produced a smile, but I don't recall if we did. The agent did not.

He was furious when he discovered we had been mailed the incorrect set of keys, as he had to leave his master keys with us. Often I'm unsure if it's an advantage or disadvantage when you don't speak another language. In this case, I was sure it was an advantage as the look on the agent's face put fear in my heart.

With two weeks in Paris, a week on the Canal du Midi, three weeks in Provence, and a return to Paris for a few days before flying home—we consumed a lot of duck. All the duck meals were good but none came close to our first duck meal in Versailles.

Another seven years passed as we traveled to other countries and on other adventures until Paris and the perfect duck meal clamored once again to the top of our list.

This trip was even longer—a few days in Giverny, eight days in Normandy, two weeks in the Loire Valley, a month in the Languedoc region and finally wrapping up the trip with two weeks in Paris.

Everywhere we traveled, we ate duck—some okay, some good, some delicious—but not one compared to that perfect duck meal in Versailles. Twenty-six years had passed since that meal. We had had many exceptional meals around the world.

And while we were still hoping for a repeat of our best duck meal in Versailles, we did have the best meal that we have ever eaten in our lives sans duck. L'oustau de Baumanière is a three-starred Michelin restaurant in Les Baux-de-Provence. It was one of those serendipity moments in life. We had just left a fabulous but rather dusty light show featuring the work of famous Renaissance artists illuminated on the walls of a quarry. We highly recommend that you experience this if you're in the area. We were dressed for the quarry and not for a three-star restaurant. But the maître d' never faltered and seated us on the terrace—a table with a view over the gardens and fountains. Duck wasn't on the menu or we would have ordered it. But it was the perfect meal ever and years later we still discuss the menu, the ambiance, Maître d'hôtel (who was incredibly kind to two grubby Americans), and the chef who packaged up complimentary desserts for us when we didn't order any.

Once back in Paris in our lovely apartment in the seventh arrondissement, the search for the next perfect duck meal began. The search continued until the very last day. On the off-chance that a very popular cafe close to our apartment might take walk-ins, we ventured out. La Fontaine De Mars is a well known local restaurant that became famous after the Obama's dined here on June 10, 2009. We had no clue until we were seated and a large sign said *Obama a dîné chez une tarbaise!*

This restaurant had been recommended to us as one of the best places for confit de canard in the 7th arrondissement. Because we didn't have reservations, we promised ourselves that we would not be upset if we were turned away. Instead, the head waiter apologized that there were only two "house" tables available and the locations were less than desirable. But we were welcomed to either.

We chose the small table against the wall where we could see into the open kitchen. Since we formerly owned a restaurant and did all the cooking, we loved to watch all the hustle and bustle in a well-run kitchen. Once we were seated, we examined the red-checkered table cloth and the napkins which were large enough to cover the entire top part of my body. They were stitched with the name of the restaurant. It was delightful to know getting food on my clothes would not occur during this meal if this napkin was tucked under my chin.

We ordered the two most traditional French dishes—escargot and confit de canard with the house red. I wept with joy, and I'm sure Ray wanted to but he refrained. A French baguette was the perfect foil to sop up the buttery, garlicky sauce from the six individual slots on the escargot plate. I was truly grateful that we had each ordered our own plate. In that moment when the first bite of escargot slid into my mouth, I wanted to yell out loud that we had found the right restaurant. My thoughts fast-forwarded to the duck feast that I was anticipating. It was sure to be phenomenal. It was.

The duck dish arrived with a flourish that only Parisians can pull off, a large white plate centered with a succulent leg and thigh of duck, surrounded by roasted and browned potatoes and a lovely endive salad seasoned with salt, pepper, lemon, and olive oil. Our knives slid through the crispy crackle of the skin. We paused, nodded, smiled and dug into the perfectly tender, falling off the bones duck.

Friends often asked us why we didn't return to restaurant in Versailles where we had our first perfect duck meal. Wasn't it logical that we'd return?

Maybe that's what other people do? I only know we don't. Our motto was and continues to be that you can never return to a certain time, place, experience, taste, smell, and touch—for us these perfect events cannot be recreated. We had that moment, and we savored it with all our being. And now, we've had the second moment. We released the goodness of these meals to the universe for another sojourner to experience.

It's always our goal to one day return to Paris—perhaps for our fortieth anniversary which is looming large in 2023. Will we eat duck? Of course, we will.

Mission Accomplished

(3 WAYS TO READ POEM)
MINOTI VAISHNAV

snow fluttered down like cold magic
in Paris on Christmas eve.
under bright lights,
I realized the city was
a true yuletide wonderland.
I entered my vacation rental…
at peace with my loneliness.
suddenly, there was movement…
in an old tree – merely a foot away from
me! a creature drew alarmingly near.
what was it?
just a sweet dog at my window!
I found his collar. JACQUES, it read.
he lived in a building –
a flat right across the road.
"come on, little dog," I said.
I took him to his abode.
I rode the elevator to the 2nd floor and
I wondered who Jacques's human was.
ah! here was what I was looking for.
the flat had a green door. *ding dong.*
a handsome Frenchman lived here.
he invited me inside…
to sit on his new couch,
and suddenly I felt warm.
as I drank from an old mug,
the cunning puppy wagged his tail…
he was happy for our union.

as I arrived
in the famed City of Love
I felt sad and cynical. then suddenly,
full of renewed possibility…
I found the holiday spirit and warmed up.
sitting at my window seat I felt
content. I gazed at the Arc de Triomphe…until
I spied a shadow on a branch outside
my window. oh dear…
I sat frozen in fear!
ah! it was only a labrador puppy.
he climbed onto the sill. I looked for identification.
oh! his name was Jacques.
44 Rue de Tilsitt. *L'appartement* 24 was his home…
I petted him and smiled.
"your owner must be worried."
the building across the street was fancy.
as I walked down the hall, I was curious…
was the dog's owner kind? was Jacques happy?
I stopped in front of 24.
I rang the doorbell. the door opened…
the owner! his eyes lit up when he saw Jacques.
he had only just moved in. he planned
to watch the snow outside his window and relax.
he made us eggnog.
Jacques looked up at us.
this was his plan all along. no more loneliness…
mission accomplished.

.

About Our Contributors

Sylvie R. Bordzuk is the author of two children's picture books, The Adventures of Kodie and Bella and Mystery at Sea - A Noah's Ark Tale (both Red Penguin publications), and also enjoys writing poetry. She is a former teacher of French and Spanish and has held a variety of executive assistant positions over the years. Her passions are reading, writing, tutoring, music, and everything having to do with animals - the latter being the inspiration for much of her writing. She is currently working on a sequel to The Adventures of Kodie and Bella and a book of poetry.

———

Katrenia Grace Busch is a freelance journalist, poet, and writer. Her poem, "Mystery & Wind" was awarded 2nd place in the Spring 2022 League for Innovation Creative Writing Contest. She sits on an editorial board for the American Psychological Association and some of her publications can be found in 50 Give or Take, Bloom Magazine, Red Penguin Books, October Hill, The Trouvaille Review among others.

———

Vanessa Caraveo is an award-winning bilingual author, published poet, and artist who has a passion for promoting inclusion, empowerment and equality for all, helping others discover the power they possess within themselves to overcome adversity and persevere in life. She is involved with various organizations that assist children and adults with disabilities and enjoys working with non-profit groups and volunteering in the promotion of literacy. Vanessa aspires to continue making a positive difference in many lives through her service to others and literary work.

David Clémenceau is of French and German origins and has an MA in translation. His work has been published in print and online in USA, UK, Canada and India and can be found in literary venues such as Idle Ink, ActiveMuse, Nzuri Journal of Coastline College and Welter at University of Baltimore, among others. He lives in Germany where he teaches secondary school English and thinks and writes mostly in English.

Alter Egos was first published in Tigershark Magazine (Tigershark Publishing, December 2020, issue 28, The Festive Season) and Twist & Twain (February 2021).

Facebook: David Clémenceau Author

Twitter: DavidCl3menceau

Instagram: dvd_42_dc_writer

Kathryn Cockrill is an author and poet from the East of England. Her first collection of short stories, Case Files of the Supernatural, was published in 2018 and her first YA novel was published in 2021. She was recently featured in They Call Us Damsels with her poem Sweet Cyanide and in Red Penguin's London anthology, 'London: Smokes, Blokes and Jokes of Foggy Town'. When she's not writing, Kathryn can be found drinking bubble tea, baking or cuddling her two dogs, Tofu and Biscuit.

Linda Trott Dickman is an award winning poet, author of four chapbooks and a poetry prompt book for children of all ages. Her work has been anthologized locally and internationally. She is the coordinator of poetry for the Northport Arts Coalition. Linda works with poets of all ages, at the Walt Whitman Birthplace Association, local museums, and leads a poetry workshop at Samantha's Li'l Bit O' Heaven coffee house. Linda makes a linguine and clam sauce recipe that is as old as she is. She loves singing in her church choir. She is a punster.

Carolyn (C.S.) Donnell has been published in anthologies and won awards in fiction, poetry, and memoir from San Francisco Writers Conference, San Mateo County Fair Literary Arts, and more. Also two novels (under C. S. Donnell). CWC South Bay's 2018 Matthews-Baldwin service award and CWC's 2019 Jack London Award.

https://www.amazon.com/C-S-Donnell/e/B017GGDZTI

https://carolyndonnell.wordpress.com

Joseph A Farina is a retired lawyer in Sarnia, Ontario, Canada. An award winning poet .Internationally published in Europe and Middle East. published in Quills Canadian Poetry Magazine, Ascent ,Subterranean Blue and in The Tower Poetry Magazine, Inscribed, The Windsor Review, Boxcar Poetry Revue , and appears in the anthologies Sweet Lemons: Writings with a Sicilian Accent, canadian Italians at Table, Witness and Tamaracks: Canadian Poetry for the 21st Century . published in U.S. magazines Mobius, Pyramid Arts, Arabesques, Fiele-Festa, Philedelphia

Poets and Memoir and in Silver Birch Press Series. He has had two books of poetry published— The Cancer Chronicles and The Ghosts of Water Street and an E-book Sunsets in Black and White. and his latest book,The beach, the street and everything in between.

Elaine Gilmartin writes: I am a therapist by profession, which is a great career for writers because I get into people's heads and hear stories that can seem too fantastic even for fiction. It's also helpful in that it is my job to challenge how they perceive themselves and the world around them, not always an easy task! I write articles for the online site Medium and love to start each day with a long run. Adventure and travel are my passions, especially if it involves melty cheese.

Ken Goldman, former Philadelphia teacher of English and Film Studies, is an Active member of the Horror Writers Association. He has homes on the Main Line in Pennsylvania and at the Jersey shore. His stories have appeared in over 970 independent press publications in the U.S., Canada, the UK, and Australia with over twenty due for publication in 2023. Since 1993 Ken's tales have received seven honorable mentions in The Year's Best Fantasy & Horror. He has written six books : three anthologies of short stories, YOU HAD ME AT ARRGH!! (Sam's Dot Publishers), DONNY DOESN'T LIVE HERE ANYMORE (A/A Productions) and STAR-CROSSED (Vampires 2); and a novella, DESIREE, (Damnation Books). His first novel OF A FEATHER (Horrific Tales Publishing) was released in January 2014. SINK-HOLE, his second novel, was published by Bloodshot Books August 2017.

Mark Andrew Heathcote is adult learning difficulties support worker. He has poems published in journals, magazines, and anthologies both online and in print. He resides in the UK and is from Manchester. Mark is the author of "In Perpetuity" and "Back on Earth," two books of poems published by Creative Talents Unleashed.

Patricia Conor Hodapp is the author of *The Bucket List, 100 Things to do in Santa Fe*. Patricia's librarian skills help her to discover hidden places, and the interactions with everyone around her gives her entry to the real residents of city she is exploring. Retired from the directorship of the Santa Fe NM public libraries, writing and painting are her passions.

Gerald Everett Jones holds a Bachelor of Arts with Honors from the College of Letters, Wesleyan University. He is the award-winning author of 13 novels, including the romantic comedy "Mick & Moira & Brad, literary fiction "Harry Harambee's Kenyan Sundowner," the Preacher Evan Wycliff mystery-thriller series, and the psychological literary novel "Clifford's Spiral." He wrote a series of three satiric Rollo Hemphill misadventures, the adult melodrama "Christmas Karma," the crime story "Choke Hold," the father-son comedy "Mr. Ballpoint," and the historical thriller "Bonfire of the Vanderbilts." He co-authored the nonfiction memoir "The Light in His Soul: Lessons from My Brother's Schizophrenia." He has also written more than 25 nonfiction books on business and technical subjects, including the bestselling "How to Lie with Charts." He is an award-winning screenwriter. He serves on the board of the Independent Writers of Southern

California (IWOSC) and is the host of the GetPublished! Radio podcast. Learn more at geraldeverettjones.com.

Suzanne Kamata first went to Paris while on foreign study as a student at the University of South Carolina. A dedicated francophile, she has written about Paris in her novel Gadget Girl: The Art of Being Invisible (GemmaMedia, 2013), which was awarded the Paris Book Festival Grand Prize, and her memoir Squeaky Wheels: Travels with my Daughter by Train, Plane, Metro, Tuktuk and Wheelchair (Wyatt-Mackenzie Publishing, 2014), winner of a Silver Nautilus Book Award. Her most recent novel is The Baseball Widow (Wyatt-Mackenzie Publishing, 2021), which is set in Japan.

David Lange was born and grew up on Long Island, New York. A graduate of the United States Air Force Academy, he served for 30 years as an Active Duty officer in the United States Air Force before retiring in 2018. Colonel Lange is a decorated combat veteran and flew numerous combat, combat support, and humanitarian relief missions during his career. He was awarded the prestigious Institute of Navigation Superior Achievement Award in recognition of his life-long accomplishments as a practicing navigator. David loves sharing stories of hope and inspiration. He has numerous short stories, essays, and poems published within various anthologies and his memoir, "Quest: My Journey Through La Mancha," was published in 2020.

Kim Poulos Lieberz is the CEO, and entrepreneurial spirit of KGI Design Group. KGI is a certified WBE and DBE, woman-owned creative agency, which has been creating multi-media strategically branded marketing and rendering solutions for over 29 years. Kim is a proud summa cum laude graduate of SUNY FIT, attended Yale University's Brissago program, and is a graduate of Goldman Saks 10KSB business growth cohort.

Kim consistently gives back to the community and, with KGI, donates funds and services to many not-for-profit organizations. As the daughter of a veteran she supports veterans groups and acts as a guardian for Honor Flight. She has supported the Rett syndrome community since 1994 and has been working with the American Cancer Society on multiple NYC distinguished events since 2015. Kim has been the emcee for St Baldrick's for many years, supporting pediatric cancer research. She is a recent town of Oyster Bay and NYS Woman of Distinction and Long Island Business News Corporate Citizen Honoree.

Kim is the co-creator and owner of BarnyardLaneSignCo.com and a founding board member of the interior design industry not-for-profit DesignGivers.org. She is grateful for her super-supportive husband of over 32 years, Scott, her dog Macy, and her two sons, Nicholas and Vincent, who spent many years trying to hide from Kim's next big idea, but who have embraced their mom's spirit as adults.

Rex McGregor is a New Zealand playwright. His short comedies have been produced on four continents from New York and London to Sydney and Chennai.

Website: https://www.rexmcgregor.com/

Colleen Moyne is a South Australian-based writer, currently travelling full-time in a van with her greyhound, Winter.

Her poems and stories have appeared in over forty different collections, both in Australia and overseas. Her work has appeared on both the 'Tales to Terrify' and 'Creepy' podcasts.

Colleen's first solo collection, 'Time Like Coins,' was published in 2018, and her second, 'Called to Coddiwomple' in 2023.

She received the Mindshare Australia 'Open Your Mind' Poetry Award and placed second in the Ken Vincent Poetry Award. Her first book, 'Time Like Coins' was nominated for an Anne Elder Award.

———

Wendy Jones Nakanishi, an American by birth, spent thirty-six years living and working in Japan. She is now dividing her retirement between the UK and Japan. She has published widely on Japanese and English literature and, under the pen name of Lea O'Harra, is the author of the Inspector Inoue mystery series set in rural modern-day Japan: Imperfect Strangers (2015); Progeny (2016); and Lady First (2017), originally published by Endeavour Press and recently reissued by Sharpe Books. She has also just published a standalone murder mystery set in small-town America: Dead Reckoning (2022).

———

Bhavya Prabhakar is a visiting lecturer by profession hailing from India. She teaches French language in India at Delhi University. She has obtained a Master's Degree in French Literature, which has provided her with many opportunities. A poet at heart, she started writing for Poet's Corner that further aroused her passion and zeal for writing. Some of her poems have been published in Indian Periodical, Spillwords Press (New York), Free Verse Revolution, The Writers and Readers' Magazine, Muse India, Too Well Away Literary Journal and Culture Cult. Recently, she published her debut poetry book, Water and Wine.

William John Rostron's books have a readership that spans five continents and all fifty states. His series of novels steeped in the late 20th and early 21st centuries' music and culture, Band in the Wind, Sound of Redemption, and Brotherhood of Forever, have received critical acclaim from Writers Digest, the Online Book Club Review, and have consistently received Amazon ratings of 4.5 out of 5, or higher. He recently added to this series with The Other Side of the Wind, a book that may be read either independently of the series or in addition to it. He has published over three dozen short stories in anthologies, five receiving awards from Writers Digest this year. Most of these pieces appear in his short story compilation, A Flamingo Under the Carousel. Five of his stories have been produced on the New York stage and are available for viewing on the author's website. www.WilliamJohn-Rostron.com

Born and raised in Queens, NY, William John Rostron now splits his time between his home on Long Island and traveling the country in his Tiffin motorhome. He is busy completing a bucket list of travel adventures when not writing. In the past 19 years, he and his wife, Marilyn, have traveled 150,000 miles. These journeys have taken them to the 48 contiguous states, 133 national parks, all 30 major league baseball stadiums, 154 cities and towns, two Canadian provinces, and various unusual experiences and locations. Many of these locations have served as backgrounds for his books.

He is presently working on a second book of short stories tentatively titled T-Rex Stole My Computer and a fifth novel in the Cambria Band in the Wind series, Dancing with the Lost.

www.WilliamJohnRostron.com

Annette Towler was born in England and moved to America in the early 1990s. She has written several poetry books, novels and murder mysteries. Annette is a therapist and enjoys running in her spare time. She lives in a house in Shorewood, Wisconsin with her partner, Gardner, and a sweet cat called Marsha.

Jasmine Tritten is an award-winning author born in Denmark. In 1964 she immigrated to the U.S.A. The last five years she has written numerous short stories published in various anthologies. Her memoir The Journey of an Adventuresome Dane, published in 2015, won an award. A children's story, Kato's Grand Adventure, published in 2018, she wrote with her husband. It won five awards. During the pandemic in 2020, Jasmine wrote and self-published a travel book On the Nile with a Dancing Dane that won three awards in 2021. Jasmine resides in enchanting Corrales, New Mexico with her husband and four cats.

Minoti Vaishnav is a television writer best known for her work on the CBS television shows THE EQUALIZER and TRUE LIES. As a short fiction author and poet, her work has appeared in several print anthologies and literary magazines. Minoti has a Masters degree in Creative Writing from the University of Oxford. She lives in Los Angeles.

Eva Zimmerman, born in Paris, left with her parents at a very young age. She longed to re-visit her birthplace. Most of all, she wanted to walk along the Blvd. Montparnasse then turn the corner into the street into which she had lived. Seeing the street, the building, the courtyard in which she had once played, meant more to her than the myriad of landmarks and attractions, beautiful though they were. Eva's visit back to Paris made her feel as if she had come full circle. Her dream of returning, at last realized.